Love, Power, and Justice

BY WILLIAM HATCHER

Bahá'í Publishing Trust

Wilmette, Illinois 60091

Bahá'í Publishing Trust, Wilmette, Illinois 60091-2886

Copyright © 1998, 2002 by William Hatcher
All rights reserved. Second edition 2002.
Printed in the United States of America
Printed on acid-free paper ∞

08 07 06 05   5 4 3

Library of Congress Cataloging-in-Publication Data
Hatcher, William S.
     Love, power, and justice / by William Hatcher.—2nd ed.
         p. cm.
     Includes bibliographical references and index.
     ISBN 0-87743-289-9 (alk. paper)
        1. Bahai ethics. 2. Bahai Faith—Doctrines. 3. Authenticity
     (Philosophy) I. Title.
BJ1288 .H38 2002
297.9'35—dc21

                                          2001043467

To my Russian friends,
with affection and gratitude

Table of Contents

Love, Power, and Justice

Preface to the Second Edition

The first edition of *Love, Power, and Justice* presented the outlines of a theory of morality based on the notion of authentic relationships between the self and reality. Such relationships are progressive and derive from an increasingly accurate perception of the structure of reality coupled with a conscious will to act on the basis of this perception. Our relationships become inauthentic when our knowledge is faulty or incomplete, or when, for whatever reason, we lack the will or the motivation to act on our knowledge.

According to the Bahá'í teachings, God has ordained two sources of valid knowledge of reality: science and revelation.[1] The object of knowledge is the same in both cases, but the methods are different. Science operates by systematizing the otherwise spontaneous experience of concrete reality and, by inductive generalization coupled with creative conceptualization, moving upward toward abstract, general principles (laws), which are then tested through further experience by the systematic application of certain *verification procedures*. The language of science is deliberately *linear*—eschewing metaphor and multiple meaning—and *minimalist*—accepting the objective existence of only those nonobservables strictly necessary to an explanation of observable configurations (which, as it turns out, is still quite a bit). Thus, the strengths of science are clarity, precision, and applicability (practicality). Its limitations derive

---

1. See 'Abdu'l-Bahá, *Paris Talks*, nos. 44:23–26.

primarily from its partialness (specialization, fragmentation), relative incompleteness, and general lack of a global vision.[2]

Revelation, based on the divine authority of the Manifestation, is the perfect complement to science. In contrast to the language of science, the language of revelation is *nonlinear* (extensive use of metaphor and multiple meaning) and *maximalist* (as rich as possible, freely referring to nonobservables). Moreover, Bahá'u'lláh repeatedly affirms that His revelation is a complete (though nonlinear and inexhaustible) description of the structure and dynamics of reality, and that even one word from His pen is capable of effecting a worldwide revolution in human understanding.[3]

Also in contrast to the language of science, the language of revelation tends to be "top-down"—beginning with certain very general and universal principles and then moving by specification and individuation toward the application of these principles to concrete human experience. Thus, the strengths of revelation are its adequacy and its completeness; its limitations (from the human point of view) lie in its complexity and the consequent frequent lack of an obvious linear meaning for a given portion of the revelatory text. The student of revelation must be prepared to struggle to understand the different levels of meaning enfolded in the revelation.

To sum up: the study of science consists in confronting our experience of the phenomena of reality, formulating certain proposi-

---

2. The original program of modern science, as conceived by Descartes and his successors, was to generate a complete description of reality in exact, mathematical language. The initial success of Newton's *Principia*, followed by the 19th century accomplishments of Maxwell, and then Darwin and his successors, raised expectations that such a daring program might in fact succeed. However, Heisenberg's uncertainty principle in physics, followed by Gödel's incompleteness theorem in mathematics and logic, and, finally, Penrose's strong thesis regarding the indeterminacy of the human brain have utterly destroyed any faintly reasonable hope of the program's success. There is an inescapable trade-off between exactness, on the one hand, and completeness, on the other. In choosing exactness, science has thereby renounced completeness.

3. See Bahá'u'lláh, *Gleanings from the Writings of Bahá'u'lláh*, p. 175; Bahá'u'lláh, *Tablets of Bahá'u'lláh*, pp. 140–41; and, Bahá'u'lláh, quoted in Shoghi Effendi, *World Order of Bahá'u'lláh*, pp. 107 and 109.

tions whose meaning is a priori clear (because of the linearity of scientific language), and applying appropriate verification procedures to determine the truth or falsity of these propositions. We call this whole process *verification* for short. Studying the revelation consists in confronting various portions of the text of revelation, focusing on certain statements whose truth is known a priori, and then striving to determine various linear meanings of these statements. We will give the name *explication* to this process (meaning to "make explicit" the meanings of the text). Thus, for science, clarity of meaning is given a priori but truth is determined a posteriori. For (revealed) religion, truth is given a priori, but meaning is determined a posteriori.

The persistent, conjoint application of scientific verification on the one hand and careful and prayerful explication of revelation on the other yields the very thing we need for the successful prosecution of the human enterprise: truth; accurate, useful, and adequate knowledge of reality. We may reasonably conclude, therefore, that the method of Bahá'í scholarship is the systematic, judicious, and disciplined application, to the data of reality, of the twin processes of scientific verification and textual explication (most particularly applied to the texts of the Bahá'í revelation).

This is the method that has been applied by a small (but international) group of researchers, established simultaneously with the publication of the first edition of *Love, Power, and Justice*. This group, now formally constituted as the Authenticity Project, has devoted its efforts to the elaboration, application, implementation, and pedagogy of the basic parameters of authenticity and its pursuit. Gradually a body of material has been generated, refined, and tested through several pilot courses and seminars given both to Bahá'ís and to non-Bahá'ís. The group intends to publish this material in workbook form and in staged segments. The first segment, currently under the working title of *Inner Freedom and Self-Mastery: The Dynamics of Moral Authenticity*, should be available in the near future.

All segments of the workbook material revolve around a central theme/process called "the virtuous cycle." A brief exposition of the current form of the virtuous cycle is contained in appendix III of the present, second edition of *Love, Power, and Justice*. We have thus been able to maintain the second edition of *Love, Power, and Justice* as the ongoing conceptual basis of the Authenticity Project.

The current members of the so-called core group of the Authenticity Project are: Leslie Asplund, Carmel Davey-Hatcher, Sheri Dressler, William Hatcher, Lonya Osokin, Michael Penn, and Mary K. Radpour. Both the present author, and the other members of the Authenticity Project, would like to express our individual and collective thanks to the Bahá'í Publishing Trust for facilitating the expeditious publication of the second edition of *Love, Power, and Justice*. Particular thanks are due to Ladan Cockshut, who was the editor for both the first and second editions. Her devoted attention to every aspect of the production has contributed immensely to the quality of the final product. Terry Cassiday should likewise be thanked for her continuing support during all stages of the process.

WILLIAM HATCHER
QUEBEC, CANADA
JULY 2001

Preface to the First Edition

This work is a slightly revised and enlarged version of the monograph, *The Ethics of Authenticity*, first published in limited edition by the International Moral Education Project, St. Petersburg, Russia, in June, 1997. The labor involved in producing the original monograph was considerably more than had been initially anticipated, but this investment of time and energy rendered less difficult the generation of the revisions and extensions necessary to produce the present volume. As it now stands, our work has greater scope and vision than at the beginning, and so one has the feeling that the various efforts were worthwhile.

The conception that *authentic morality* is based on the pursuit of authentic relationships between the self and various aspects of reality was present from the start, but some of its deeper implications emerged only later. In developing our program or system of ethics, we have freely drawn on three major sources of knowledge: science, philosophy, and religion, in particular (but not exclusively) the teachings and writings of the Bahá'í Faith. However, a certain number of the concepts and ideas are, as far as we know, original—in the precise sense that we have not consciously or deliberately borrowed them from other sources.

Any discussion of the origins of the major concepts of our ethical system would generate another book. However a bit of historical perspective may be helpful. We have gradually converged on the realization that the overall structure of reality can be effectively and usefully analyzed in terms of the three fundamental, binary relations of causality, composition, and value. Each of these is viewed as a relationship between *phenomena*, where a phenomenon is defined as some portion of total reality (though value must be restricted to that narrower class of phenomena called *entities*). Speaking very roughly (begging the reader's indulgence at this point), causality is epistemology, composition is metaphysics, and value is ethics and aesthetics.

There appears to be a vigorous history of studying each of these relationships separately (e.g., Aristotle's well-known study of causation), but the study of the logical connections between them appears less well developed (though there are a few precedents). Our approach to these questions relies heavily on the modern logic of relations but, as it turns out, has strong roots in the work of the great Muslim philosopher, physician, and mathematician, Avicenna.[1] Some of the logical properties governing these principles and their interconnections can be found in chapter 3, section 4, on the existence and nature of God. In the present work, we have given only the barest outlines of this logic, so as to avoid blurring the focus of the exposition and rendering it unnecessarily complicated for the reader unfamiliar with these notions. However, a more detailed axiomatic approach exists and will be published at a later date.

Many people should be thanked for their help: Farzam Arbab and Douglas Martin for suggesting the project in the first place; the Office of Social and Economic Development of the Bahá'í International Community for its financial assistance; Paul Lample for his support and encouragement, and for kindly accepting to write the introduction; Vadim Nomokonov and Leonid Osokin for their con-

---

1. Avicenna is the Westernized form of the name of ibn Sina (980–1037), one of the great thinkers produced by the Islamic tradition. Avicenna was accomplished in mathematics, medicine, philosophy, and theology. He began his life's work by thoroughly assimilating and mastering the Hellenic intellectual heritage, particularly Aristotle. He then made creative contributions of his own to philosophy, based on insights gained from the Qu'ran, the Muslim holy book. His work on proofs of the existence and nature of God were precociously modern, prefiguring methods and concepts that entered into the mainstream of philosophy and mathematics only in the late nineteenth century. See William Hatcher, "Causality, Composition, and the Origin of Existence" (in John Hatcher and William Hatcher, *The Law of Love Enshrined*) where a detailed treatment and appropriate references are given.

stant collaboration on all aspects of the program; the students and administration of those various Russian universities which have generously given me the opportunity to present appropriately selected versions of the material in course form, contributing thereby to its development; my wife Judith for her painstaking review of the entire manuscript. There are many others, but I hope they will accept my collective thanks. All limitations in the program should be attributed to the author and not to any of these collaborators or assistants.

WILLIAM S. HATCHER
QUEBEC, CANADA
17 SEPTEMBER 1997

Introduction

Today there is no more pressing problem confronting humanity than determining those precepts that can lead to the establishment of just and moral relations among individuals and nations. Though the dominant ideologies that have recklessly consumed millions of lives in the twentieth century have largely burned themselves out, their end offers little relief to humanity, but seems only to have left the ground clear for the thorns of tribal conflict and the weeds of moral anarchy. If there is any hope for the establishment of a new social order, it lies in the convergence of thought about a universal system of morals based on a shared understanding of reality. For just as the diverse peoples and cultures of the world have been united in their embrace of the universal truths of science—one never speaks of "Canadian" physics, "Egyptian" physics, or "Chinese" physics—so too can they be united in a global community through a moral system which is the product of a collective search for truth.

In his seminal text, *After Virtue*, Alasdaire MacIntyre concludes that the attempts of modern philosophy to deal with questions of morality have been a catastrophic failure. Left only with the fragments of discourse remaining from an ancient morality once grounded in meaningful social context, modern moral reasoning and discussion are reduced to endless debates in which rival premises are never truly engaged. MacIntyre observes that moral conversation has become a clash of ever more vehement assertions and counter assertions that cannot be resolved except by appeal to emotion. Such an intractable situation reinforces the widespread belief that morality falls totally under the rule of subjectivism and relativism.

Although MacIntyre offers an insightful critique of the moral dilemma faced by contemporary society, his proposed resolution lies largely in a return to the past and an exploration of tradition. Such nostalgia, his critics have maintained, is "an evasion of the problems of modernity, not a solution to them." As Ross Poole notes:

> The starting point of the quest is our ignorance of the good. But this ignorance may be interpreted in two ways. It may be that we do not know what our good is because we lack a certain item of knowledge. Our quest for the good life is a search in a literal sense: it aims to discover (or rediscover) something which already exists. We are like archaeologists trying to discover the plan of a city hidden beneath the rubble of history. Our good is the pre-established unity of our life; our task is to find out what it is and to live it. However, another interpretation might be that we do not know what the good life is because it has to be created. We are not like archaeologists, but more like artists attempting to bring into existence something which has never existed before. When we find our good it will not be a discovery, but a creation.[1]

In this brief but thought-provoking text, Dr. William Hatcher combines the best of MacIntyre's archaeologist and Poole's artist. Building on his earlier work in the books, *Logic and Logos* and *The Law of Love Enshrined*, the author draws from science, philosophy, and religion to present a definition of morality and moral development based on specific conclusions about the nature of reality and on an understanding that the attainment of the good must always be an act of creative discovery.

Chapter 1 defines morality in terms of the establishment of a proper relationship with God, and, consequently, with other human beings, through the expression of self-sacrificing love. It recognizes within reality a value hierarchy in which God is the highest value and the human being the highest created value in existence. It dis-

---

1. Ross Poole, *Morality and Modernity*, pp. 149–150.

sects a variety of alternative approaches to morality, religious and non-religious, that sacrifice authentic human relationships to the pursuit of false values, whether by defining morality in more easily achievable terms, for example as ideology, legalism, or romanticism, or by ruthlessly promoting the view that self-worth can only be attained at the expense of others.

Chapter 2 examines moral development as a process which leads to an autonomous human being who is able to attain authentic well-being: individuals who can direct their own actions in order to achieve happiness through the fulfillment of their true nature. A detailed model is presented to suggest the means by which the capacities of the mind, heart, and will are actualized as a person's inner models of reality are refined through constant interactions with other subjects and with material objects. The law of cause and effect inherent in the universe applies, Dr. Hatcher asserts, not only to the realm of facts but also to the realm of values; when we understand how this laws works and can appropriately direct our interactions with reality, true happiness will be achieved.

Morality must, of course, go beyond moral understanding to achieve moral action. Thus, the final chapter considers the implementation of the development process. Aspects of a disciplined approach to one's relationship with God, the self, society and social groups, and the physical world are explored. The moral person is envisioned not as a finished product, but as a learner engaged in an unending but inherently rewarding enterprise.

Because the manuscript makes liberal use of concepts found in the writings of the Bahá'í Faith, readers who are Bahá'ís will find much that is familiar. Yet the author has combined these familiar concepts into an original formulation that provides fresh insights into the framework of morality enshrined in the teachings of Bahá'-u'lláh. It presents a language which can assist in a search for a universal expression of moral precepts and practices. Moreover, it offers Bahá'ís a conceptual approach to help them weigh the views inherited from their culture in the balance of their spiritual and ethical beliefs.

However, the most important contribution of this book is that it goes beyond the purely conceptual or theoretical and invites the reader to set aside the false sense of comfort and security afforded by limited approaches to morality and take up the challenge of learning to build genuine human relationships aided by the knowledge systems of science and religion. Moral development then moves from the arena of indoctrination or elaborate argumentation to a systematic exploration of experience in a variety of social or cultural settings. While the text does not explicitly present an approach to moral education, it provides stimulating material for teachers and students interested in this field.

"Moral life," 'Abdu'l-Bahá is reported to have said, "consists in the government of one's self." "Immortality"—that is, the spiritual life—"is government of a human soul by the Divine Will."[2] By assisting the reader in understanding the process of the development of human potentiality that lies embedded within the very nature of reality, Dr. Hatcher has helped, in no small measure, to narrow the gap between the good life and the eternal life.

PAUL LAMPLE
JUNE 1997

2. 'Abdu'l-Bahá, in *Ten Days in the Light of 'Akká*, p. 5.

Chapter 1

The Nature of Authentic Morality

1. The Supreme Value in Creation: the Human Being

Human moral development requires an understanding of the nature of value, both intrinsic value—arising from the inherent properties of an entity, and extrinsic value—which we attribute to an entity through subjective preferences (so-called value choices) and social conventions. An example of the latter is the value generally attributed to money, which in itself is nothing more than ink on paper, a highly ephemeral entity that quickly deteriorates into a formless mass of colored fibers.

Since intrinsic value is inherent in the very nature (essence) of any given entity (existent), it is objective. Intrinsic values define a binary *value relation* $\geq$ between entities. Thus, where A and B are two entities, we write $A \geq B$ to mean that A is as valuable as B (i.e., the intrinsic value of A is greater than or equal to the intrinsic value of B).

The ultimate source of all intrinsic values is God, for He is the Creator who has alone determined the inner structure and degree of refinement of each entity in existence. God Himself is thus the ulti-

1

mate value, the uncreated, supreme value in all existence. He is therefore the ultimate end and goal of all human moral striving. Indeed,
the Founder of the Bahá'í Faith, Bahá'u'lláh (1817–1892), affirms
that pursuit of the knowledge and love of God is the very purpose of
our existence:

> All praise to the unity of God, and all honor to Him, the sover-
> eign Lord, . . . Who, out of utter nothingness, hath created the
> reality of all things . . . Having created the world and all that
> liveth and moveth therein, He, through the direct operation of
> His unconstrained and sovereign Will, chose to confer upon
> man the unique distinction and capacity to know Him and to
> love Him—a capacity that must needs be regarded as the gen-
> erating impulse and the primary purpose underlying the whole
> of creation. . . . Upon the inmost reality of each and every cre-
> ated thing He hath shed the light of one of His names, and
> made it a recipient of the glory of one of His attributes. Upon
> the reality of man, however, He hath focused the radiance of
> all of His names and attributes, and made it a mirror of His own
> Self. Alone of all created things man hath been singled out for
> so great a favor, so enduring a bounty.[1]

Because the "reality of man" (the human soul) is capable of reflect-
ing all the attributes of God, the human being is the apex of creation, the highest created value; and the Manifestations of God (the
founders of the great religions of history), because they reflect perfectly these attributes, are the apex of humanity:

> . . . From that which hath been said it becometh evident
> that all things, in their inmost reality, testify to the revelation
> of the names and attributes of God within them. . . . Man, the
> noblest and most perfect of all created things, excelleth them
> all in the intensity of this revelation, and is a fuller expression
> of its glory. And of all men, the most accomplished, the most

---

1. Bahá'u'lláh, *Gleanings from the Writings of Bahá'u'lláh*, pp. 64–65.

distinguished, and the most excellent are the Manifestations of the Sun of Truth. Nay, all else besides these Manifestations, live by the operation of Their Will, and move and have their being through the outpourings of Their grace.[2]

Since the God-given value of humankind is inherent in our essential nature, it is intrinsic and, since it is shared by all humans, it is universal. Moral education is the process of apprehending and then expressing this value. Bahá'u'lláh explains that this is a process of development, a progressive unfolding of the God-given potential within us. The Manifestation is the source of the knowledge that drives this process.

Through the Teachings of this Day Star of Truth every man will advance and develop until he attaineth the station at which he can manifest all the potential forces with which his inmost true self hath been endowed. It is for this very purpose that in every age and dispensation the Prophets of God and His chosen Ones have appeared amongst men, and have evinced such power as is born of God and such might as only the Eternal can reveal.[3]

As Bahá'u'lláh stresses here, the very purpose and meaning of religion is the development of the highest value in creation—the intrinsic spiritual capacities of the human being. Thus defined, religion consists of a vertical relationship between God and humanity, and a lateral relationship between human beings, based on the vertical relationship each and all have with God. Since human spiritual development is the supreme value in creation, all other created values are subsidiary (and inferior) to the value of the human being and his development.

Any moral system holds that lesser values can and should be sacrificed (used as means) to obtain higher values: higher values are

---

2. Bahá'u'lláh, *Gleanings*, pp. 178–179.
3. Bahá'u'lláh, *Gleanings*, p. 68.

ends and lower values means to these ends. Thus, the essence of immorality is to confuse means and ends, thereby sacrificing higher values in the pursuit of lower ones. (A classic example is the thief, who sacrifices the higher value of authentic trustworthiness, and the lasting benefits it bestows, in order to obtain an ephemeral, often trivial, material value.)

In particular, God cannot be used as a means to obtain some other (necessarily lower) value. Since we can never actually attain to God or Godship, God has Himself ordained that the establishment of an ongoing, authentic relationship with Him represents for us the pursuit of the Divine as the ultimate value. This means that the true value of anything in creation can only be understood with reference to God. We must learn to see the Hand and Purpose of God in everything:

> . . . all things, in their inmost reality, testify to the revelation of the names and attributes of God within them. . . . "No thing have I perceived, except that I perceived God within it, God before it, or God after it."[4]

True religion is thus a living, dynamic relationship, not an ideology, a set of social conventions, or a formula for living one's life. However, these latter notions are ways in which religion and morality are often viewed. We therefore take time in the next sections to distinguish carefully between authentic morality and its various non-authentic alternatives.

2. Religion and Morality— the Pursuit of Authentic Relationships

The Being (Self) of God is the supreme value in existence and the Human Being is the supreme value in creation. *Religion* (*religia*) is the name we give to the *relationship* or link between these two values, God and humanity. The living embodiment of this link is the

---

4. Bahá'u'lláh, *Gleanings*, p. 178.

Manifestation. Religion thus consists of three fundamental components: God, Man, and the relationship between God and Man, namely the Manifestation. The fact that the Manifestation reflects perfectly the attributes of God means that the Manifestation can represent God in relation to ordinary humans. But since the Manifestation also has an individual, human soul and a physical body, He can, at the same time, represent humanity in relationship to God.[5]

Of course, everyone has a relationship to God and to other humans, whether he likes it or not. Thus, it is important to stress that true religion means a particular relationship (or quality of relationship) to God and to others, and not just any possible relationship. To distinguish true religion from other kinds of relationships, we will define true religion as the establishment of an *authentic* relationship between the self and God and between the self and other humans. Similarly, we will henceforth speak of *authentic* religion to distinguish true religion from other conceptions of the nature of religion.

Even more generally, we can say that our relationship with any given category of existence is *authentic* to the degree that it is based on an accurate perception of the structure of reality. To interact authentically with reality is thus to interact in such a way that the intrinsic and universal values embedded in reality become known to us.

Thus defined, authenticity is a generalization of the notion of validity, which occurs in science and logic, where "valid" means "in conformity with reality." However, validity is usually applied to a purely rational correspondence between certain features of reality and certain mental constructions; while we are here interested in the relationship between the totality of reality and the total person—his consciousness, mind, heart, and will.

It may seem at first that this is too broad and sweeping—that certain interactions with reality have no moral implication whatsoever. This narrow view that ethics and morality are limited only to

---

5. See the discussion of these points in *Gleanings*, and in Shoghi Effendi, *The Dispensation of Bahá'u'lláh*.

certain very specific areas of human life has been at the root of much human misery throughout history. We will see that, on the contrary, human beings are value makers and value choosers, and that questions of value and ethics are, to a greater or lesser extent, relevant to all our experiences and interactions.

Of course, it is certainly true that not all of our interactions involve the same degree of moral relevance. There is a hierarchy of ethical considerations that reflects precisely the objective, intrinsic value relation. Thus, when we interact primarily with existents of lesser value, for example rocks or minerals, this certainly has less moral implications than when we interact with more refined entities, such as other humans.

Indeed, since the human being is the supreme value in creation, it is our interactions with other humans (and with God, of course) that have the greatest degree of moral implication. So much is this so, that we can say that the most specific goal of morality is to establish authentic relationships with other human beings. We thus have the general or overall moral purpose of establishing authentic relationships with each category of existence, and the specific or particular goal of establish such relations with other human beings.

To perceive the true inner reality (intrinsic value) of a human being is to love that reality: love is our response to the recognition of value. Hence, the mark of authenticity in interhuman relationships is the presence of self-sacrificing love or *altruism*. Non-authentic relationships are based on blind attachment to a false self-perception, giving rise to various forms of egotism and self-interest. Such relationships are characterized by conflict, disharmony, manipulation, cruelty, jealousy, and the like.

Altruistic love is not just a feeling of emotional warmth towards others, but an objective, attractive force that operates according to certain objective laws and principles. Moral education means learning these laws and principles so that we become ever more subject to the force of love in our lives. Morality, then, is the *pursuit of authentic relationships* or, stated more fully, *the process of developing our innate capacity to sustain authentic relationships*.

Let us illustrate with a simple analogy from physics. Current physical theory has discovered four fundamental forces. The force of gravity and the strong nuclear force (which binds together the heavy particles of the atomic nucleus) are purely attractive. However, the weak nuclear force (which causes radioactive disintegration) is a purely repulsive force: it has no (currently known) attractive form. Finally, electro-magnetic force has both an attractive and a repulsive form. Now, the Bahá'í Writings affirm that altruistic love, like gravity, is a purely attractive force. Altruistic or authentic love *cannot* be the cause of conflict or estrangement between two people any more than the force of gravitational attraction between two physical bodies can push them apart.

Of course, physical bodies can be pulled apart by forces that overcome their mutual gravitational attraction. But, whenever we observe two physical bodies moving away from each other, we know that such a configuration is occurring in spite of their mutual gravitational attraction, not because of it. In the same way, whenever we see conflict and disharmony in human relationships, we know that this is due to some factor other than love, because love *cannot* produce estrangement. The very essence or nature of love makes it a purely attractive force.

Thus, moral development is the pursuit of relational authenticity by learning the laws that govern the action of love and then implementing this knowledge in our relationships with others. The moral person is one who has acquired the capacity for genuine love and self-sacrifice. He demonstrates this by his integrity and trustworthiness in his relations with others, by consistently treating others with genuine kindness and encouragement, by serving them and preferring their needs to his own.

In other words, the basics of morality are stark in their simplicity: either a person has acquired the capacity for self-sacrifice, which he demonstrates through active, humble, reliable service towards others, or he has not, in which case his behavior will reflect various pathologies of inauthenticity, some of which we mentioned above (e.g., greed, untrustworthiness, jealousy, self-centeredness, coldness, indifference, anger, or cruelty). It is through our actions—which reflect what we *are*—that our degree of moral development is proved out. If our actions consistently betray selfish motives, then we cannot claim that, underneath it all, we are really loving people in spite of our contrary behavior, any more than we can claim that the earth's gravity is somehow pushing airplanes into the sky.

This stark simplicity of basic morality is, of course, a challenge to every human being. To evaluate ourselves according to these criteria leads us all to painful self-revelations. Nevertheless, such self-revelations constitute the necessary first step towards authentic spirituality, and they also test the sincerity of our desire to achieve relational authenticity. The degree to which we humans have generally failed this test is reflected in a number of strategies we have devised throughout our history to transform basic morality into something else that can be more easily achieved. We now examine a few of these alternative conceptions of religion and morality.

3. Religion Viewed as Ideology

Perhaps the most pervasive alternative conception sees religion primarily as the belief in and defense of certain doctrines rather than the establishment of authentic relationships with God and others. These doctrines are viewed as the supreme value in creation, and morality is conceived as their propagation and dissemination by all possible means.

Of course, any religion presents a philosophy of life and thus teaches belief in certain doctrines and ideas. However, authentic religion considers true belief not as an end in itself but as one of the means of developing the capacity for authentic relationships. Thus, the error of ideologized religion lies not in seeking to propagate certain doctrines which it considers true, but rather in exalting these cherished doctrines above authentic relationships, thereby interchanging means and ends.

We will use the term *ideology* to designate any philosophy which holds that certain doctrines, ideas, or propositions are more important than human beings. Thus defined, any ideology (irrespective of what its specific doctrinal content may be) contradicts the basic assumption of authentic religion, which holds that the human being is the supreme value in creation. Since any moral system holds that lesser values may be sacrificed to obtain greater values, an ideology thus sanctions (at least implicitly) the deliberate sacrifice of human beings or of authentic human relationships if it is deemed necessary for the propagation of the doctrines of that ideology.

In regarding its doctrines as more important than human beings, an ideology considers these doctrines as God—as the supreme value in existence. Ideology is thus idolatry. It is the worship of certain ideas instead of the worship of God. The idolatrous nature of ideology is particularly evident in the case of certain gross political ideologies such as communism or fascism. However, religious ideologies are much more problematic since they idolatrize certain specifically religious beliefs and thus become tempting alternatives to the pursuit of relational authenticity.

The history of Christianity provides an instructive, and indeed sobering, example of the transformation of authentic religion into an ideology. Jesus Christ taught that the establishment of relational authenticity was the central purpose and true meaning of life. He said that the central commandment of religion was to love God with all one's heart and to love one's neighbor as oneself. He taught that we should love even our enemies and those who seek to harm us (after all, even a morally undeveloped person—a thief or a murderer— is capable of loving his friends). He dramatized this conception through parables and narratives in which He instructed us to "turn the other cheek" when aggressed, to "go the second mile" in deliberate self-sacrifice when forced to serve others.

Nowhere in the entire New Testament does Jesus give any doctrinal criterion of believership. Rather, He says that His true followers will be known by the fact that they "love one another; as I have loved you."[6]

The early Christian believers appear to have clearly understood the nature of true religion and to have responded positively to the challenge of pursuing relational authenticity. This is reflected in the courageous way they endured three centuries of persecution and

---

6. The Holy Bible, John 13:34.

martyrdom. Let us recall that, during this period of persecution, no social or material advantage accrued to the followers of Christ. They suffered all these persecutions uniquely for the sake of entering into relational authenticity with others. Such is the attractive power of altruistic love.

Yet, beginning with the Council of Nicea in 325 A.D.[7], the Christian Faith was gradually transformed into an ideology in which certain doctrines about the nature of Christ (so-called Christological doctrines) replaced relational authenticity as the mark of true believership. Historians tell us that, in the end, more Christians were killed by fellow Christians as a result of ideological disputes than all of the Christians killed by the Roman state during the entire period of persecution.

The ideologization of Christianity culminated in the Inquisition in which thousands upon thousands of Christian believers were put to death in the name of Jesus because they were held to deviate in some way from officially established ideology. The propagation of these doctrines was held to be more important than human beings and so human beings were sacrificed for the preservation of the doctrines. Even in the present day, it is belief in these doctrines, in some form or other, which is generally held to determine whether or not one is a true Christian.

Christianity is now the most numerous of all the major religions in the world, and we have no trouble accepting that every professed Christian truly believes in and adheres to the fundamental, established doctrines that have come to characterize Christian-

---

7. In 312 A.D., Constantine became the first Christian Emperor of the Roman Empire. After realizing the extent to which the still young Christian community was riven by theological and doctrinal differences, he ordered the first ecumenical council to be held in Nicea in the year 325 A.D. The primary issue was the metaphysical nature of Christ— whether He was identical to God or only of like nature to God. The council at Nicea voted by majority (but not unanimously) that Christ was identical to God, thus giving one precise form to the doctrine of the Trinity. This conception was then formalized in the Nicene Creed, which became the first official statement of orthodox Christian belief. However, debate on these and other theological questions continued unabated, leading to bitter antagonisms and even the spilling of Christian blood by Christians.

ity (e.g., the Divinity and Sonship of Christ, His birth by a Virgin, His resurrection from the dead). But do we dare consider how many of these same believers would pass Jesus' test of beliversfip "that ye love one another; as I have loved you."[8] Indeed, if such were the case, the whole world would be a veritable paradise of love and authenticity, given the presence of great numbers of Christian believers in every part of the globe.

Of course, Christianity is far from the only example of the transmutation of true religion into an ideology. Indeed, militant and exclusivist fundamentalist ideology seems to have now become predominant within many of the world's major religions. However, the example of Christianity is particularly instructive because the teachings of Jesus so clearly and consistently stressed altruistic love above all other considerations. Indeed, if we human beings can murder fellow believers in the name of a religion whose avowed fundamental precept is love, then we must accept that we all have within us the potential to conceive of an appropriate ideological rationalization for any cruelty whatsoever. It is the realization of this potential of our nature that should motivate us to vigilance against the ideologization of religion.

In His writings, Bahá'u'lláh consistently cautions us against such ideologization of religion:

> Oh ye that dwell on earth! The religion of God is for love and unity; make it not the cause of enmity or dissension.[9]

> The purpose of religion as revealed from the heaven of God's holy Will is to establish unity and concord amongst the peoples of the world; make it not the cause dissension and strife.[10]

In a similar vein, 'Abdu'l-Bahá (the eldest Son of Bahá'u'lláh and designated Interpreter of His Teachings) has said:

---

8. The Holy Bible, John 13:34.
9. Bahá'u'lláh, *Tablets to Bahá'u'lláh*, p. 220.
10. Bahá'u'lláh, *Tablets*, p. 129.

And among the teachings of Bahá'u'lláh is that religion must be the cause of fellowship and love. If it becomes the cause of estrangement then it is not needed, for religion is like a remedy; if it aggravates the disease then it becomes unnecessary.[11]

The third teaching of Bahá'u'lláh is that religion must be the source of fellowship, the cause of unity and the nearness of God to man. If it rouses hatred and strife, it is evident that absence of religion is preferable and an irreligious man better than one who professes it. According to the divine Will and intention religion should be the cause of love and agreement, a bond to unify all mankind for it is a message of peace and goodwill to man from God.[12]

As is clear from these statements of Bahá'u'lláh and 'Abdu'l-Bahá, and as we have already mentioned above, to say that authentic religion is not an ideology is not to say that authentic religion does not involve assent to and affirmation of certain propositions, principles, and doctrines. What it does mean is that all such doctrines should serve the moral and spiritual advancement of human beings and not that human beings, or authentic human relations, should be sacrificed for the imposition or propagation of these doctrines. Shoghi Effendi has expressed this truth as follows:

If long-cherished ideals and time-honored institutions, if certain social assumptions and religious formulae have ceased to promote the welfare of the generality of mankind, if they no longer minister to the needs of a continually evolving humanity, let them be swept away and relegated to the limbo of obsolescent and forgotten doctrines. . . . For legal standards, political and economic theories are solely designed to safeguard the interests of humanity as a whole, and not humanity to be cruci-

---

11. 'Abdu'l-Bahá, *Selections from the Writings of 'Abdu'l-Bahá*, no. 227:9.
12. 'Abdu'l-Bahá, *The Promulgation of Universal Peace*, p. 181.

fied for the preservation of the integrity of any particular law or doctrine.[13]

Ideologization is perhaps the most prevalent but unfortunately not the only distortion of authentic religion.

4. Religion Viewed as Social Convention

The presence of culture-bound elements in each of the traditional religions has led some to conclude that religion is wholly a product of culture and thus that cultural values are the only ultimate values. Many philosophical materialists add to this conception the further belief that culture itself is nothing more than the straightforward result of spontaneous interactions between a human collectivity and its immediate environment. In this view, cultural values are accidental and local rather than intrinsic and universal.

Revealed (prophetic) religion views the connection between religion and culture in exactly the opposite manner: since God is the supreme value, He is the ultimate source of all positive values, cultural or otherwise. These values are injected into human society through the revelations of the Manifestations, who represent the link (*religia*) between God and humanity. These values are partly universal and intrinsic, and partly local and extrinsic. As Bahá'u'lláh states:

> There can be no doubt whatever that the peoples of the world, of whatever race or religion, derive their inspiration from one heavenly Source, and are the subjects of one God. The difference between the ordinances under which they abide should be attributed to the varying requirements and exigencies of the age in which they were revealed. All of them, except a few which are the outcome of human perversity, were ordained of God, and are a reflection of His Will and Purpose.[14]

---

13. Shoghi Effendi, *The World Order of Bahá'u'lláh*, p. 42.
14. Bahá'u'lláh, *Gleanings*, p. 217.

These principles and laws [of revealed religion], these firmly-established and mighty systems, have proceeded from one Source, and are the rays of one Light. That they differ one from another is to be attributed to the varying requirements of the ages in which they were promulgated.[15]

As is further explained by 'Abdu'l-Bahá, the intrinsic and universal values are based on the universal nature of the human being as created and determined by God. Because there is a universal human nature, the laws, principles, and values deriving from this universal configuration are transcultural. They are thus more ultimate than any strictly cultural value. However, certain extrinsic, temporary, and local principles can serve as ancillary values to the universal ones.

> The divine religions embody two kinds of ordinances. First there are those which constitute essential, or spiritual, teachings of the Word of God. These are faith in God, the acquirement of the virtues which characterize perfect manhood, praiseworthy moralities, the acquisition of the bestowals and bounties emanating from the divine effulgences—in brief, the ordinances which concern the realm of morals and ethics. . . . This is the essential foundation of all the divine religions, the reality itself, common to all. . . .
>
> Second, there are laws and ordinances which are temporary and nonessential. These concern human transactions and relations. They are accidental and subject to change according to the exigencies of time and place. These ordinances are neither permanent nor fundamental.[16]

In sum, although there is a reciprocal relationship between culture and revealed religion, fundamentally it is revelation that produces

---

15. Bahá'u'lláh, *Gleanings*, pp. 287–288.
16. 'Abdu'l-Bahá, *Promulgation*, pp. 403–404.

culture and not the converse. The values taught by the Manifestations are mostly universal and transcultural, but are also partly local and culturally relative.

What empirical evidence is there to support the thesis that there is a universal, transcultural dimension to human nature? Quite a lot, as it turns out. If you put honey or sugar to the lips of a newly-born infant, he will respond positively and smack his lips. If you put a bitter substance such as quinine to his lips, he will recoil in evident avoidance. This response is innate and universal, and it represents that fact that there are certain stimuli to which all normally endowed humans respond positively and other stimuli to which all respond negatively. In other words, the human being has from the beginning of his life a definite internal structure, inherent in his nature, that he brings to all his encounters with reality.

This is not to deny that there are individual differences in value preferences, and that these differences are both learned and innate. The point is that the similarities between human responses to given stimuli are more important and more pervasive than the differences. All humans respond positively to love and kindness and respond negatively, by avoidance or aggression, to cruelty and pain. The fact that various cultures and peoples have found different ways of expressing both the positive value of love and the negative value of cruelty does not diminish the universality of these values themselves (whether positive or negative).

Thus authentic morality is based on the perception and knowledge of what is universal and intrinsic in human nature, and is thus transcultural, whereas culture-based moralities incorporate many arbitrary, purely subjective value preferences of particular groups or individuals.

5. Religion as a Set of Moral Rules

Yet another conception of religion is the notion that spirituality consists solely or primarily in following a set of rules for moral behavior. Of course, authentic religion has laws, precepts, duties, behavioral principles, and ethical norms, but regards these as means and not ends in themselves. Bahá'u'lláh has given a succinct but powerful statement of this truth:

> Whatever duty Thou has prescribed unto Thy servants of extolling to the utmost Thy majesty and glory is but a token of Thy grace unto them, that they may be enabled to ascend unto the station conferred upon their own inmost being, the station of the knowledge of their own selves.[17]

Legalism is the name usually given to the view which holds that religion can be reduced to a set of moral regulations. Legalism considers certain rules, and obedience to them, as the supreme value in creation in a similar manner that ideology considers belief in certain doctrines the supreme value. Relational authenticity involves the whole person, his mind, his heart and his will. It involves right understanding or thought, right feeling or motivation (altruistic love), and right action or justice. Legalism focuses on the observable action and neglects or diminishes the requirement of altruistic motivation. It therefore leads to hypocrisy (insincerity) because it allows a person to claim that he is authentically spiritual if he accomplishes acts in conformity with ethical norms, even if his inner motivation is purely selfish and even aggressively cruel. In the Kitáb-i-Aqdas, Bahá'u'lláh warns us against such presumptuous hypocrisy:

> Make not your deeds as snares wherewith to entrap the object of your aspiration, and deprive not yourselves of this Ultimate Objective for which have ever yearned all such as have drawn nigh unto God. Say: The very life of all deeds is My good pleasure, and all things depend upon Mine acceptance.[18]

The New Testament records that Jesus Christ persistently denounced the legalism of the Pharasaic Jews as a major distortion of authentic religion, just as the Qur'án of Muhammad denounces the idolatrous

---

17. Bahá'u'lláh, *Gleanings*, pp. 4–5.
18. Bahá'u'lláh, *Kitáb-i-Aqdas*, para. no. 36.

nature of certain Christological doctrines as an "adding [of] gods to God."[19] Moreover, just as the ideologization of religion serves to replace relational authenticity by the more easily achievable goal of passive belief, so legalism accomplishes a similar shift of focus: it allows the individual to avoid facing the most basic issue involved in the struggle to achieve relational authenticity—the question of purity of motive.

Shoghi Effendi has also stressed the importance of a pure and heartfelt motivation for the achievement of authenticity in our relationship with God:

> . . . the core of religious faith is that mystic feeling which unites man with God. . . . The Bahá'í Faith, like all other Divine Religions, is thus fundamentally mystic in character.[20]

The primacy and universality of love as the basis for authentic spirituality is affirmed by 'Abdu'l-Bahá in the following passage:

> Know thou of a certainty that Love is the secret of God's holy Dispensation, the manifestation of the All-Merciful, the fountain of spiritual outpourings. Love is heaven's kindly light, the Holy Spirit's eternal breath that vivifieth the human soul. Love is the cause of God's revelation unto man, the vital bond inherent, in accordance with the divine creation, in the realities of things. Love is the one means that ensureth true felicity both in this world and the next. Love is the light that guideth in darkness, the living link that uniteth God with man, that assureth the progress of every illumined soul. Love is the most great law that ruleth this mighty and heavenly cycle . . . Love revealeth with unfailing and limitless power the mysteries latent in the universe.[21]

---

19. See The Qur'án, verse 28:87; also 5:76–77.

20. Shoghi Effendi, quoted in *Spiritual Foundations: Prayer, Meditation, and the Devotional Attitude*, p. 14.

21. 'Abdu'l-Bahá, *Selections from the Writings of 'Abdu'l-Bahá*, no. 12:1.

In spite of these strong statements, there is nevertheless a tendency for us to fall into legalism, especially when it comes to moral education. This is partly because ethical norms are more objective and thus relatively easy to teach, at least on a superficial level. However, it is also because, for the most part, we have not yet learned how to teach authentic spirituality in its full dimension; the teaching of moral rules is thus seen as the best available substitute.

6. Romanticism in Religion

Ideologization and legalism represent a relative overvaluation of certain ideas and certain actions respectively. A similar overvaluation of the subjective feelings commonly experienced in altruistic love represents yet another deviation from authenticity.

Romanticism holds that the subjective feeling of euphoria and joy which accompanies altruistic love is the highest value in creation. This is perhaps the most subtle of the classical idolatries, because it can occur only when someone has already begun to develop his capacity for authenticity. It thus becomes a seductive alternative to the continued pursuit of relational authenticity, a pursuit that may always be satisfying but not always easy or pleasant.

Ideologization and legalism each make one of the means of attaining authenticity into the end, whereas romanticism takes a by-product or consequence of authenticity to be authenticity itself. Since the presence of altruistic love is the mark of relational authenticity, feelings of joy and exaltation are always present in an authentic relation. It thus becomes very easy, especially at first, to mistake these feelings of love for the love itself. One then begins to pursue the feelings for their own sake and gradually to sacrifice authenticity in the process. This is the classic "falling in love with love," but in the religious context.

The crudest but clearest example of this process is drug addiction in which one provokes temporary feelings of euphoria and well-being by artificially stimulating those areas of the brain and nervous system involved in the experience of these emotions. But, generally speaking, romantic subversion of authenticity is far more subtle; romanticism is a powerful generator of subtle illusions.

The whole history of mysticism is tinged with romantic elements, but the culmination of the romantic approach to authenticity was probably Persian Sufism. Sufi mystics held that the only mark of authenticity was a romantic euphoria called "love madness" in which one totally abandons the mind and the will to overpowering feelings of spiritual joy and euphoria.

In such works as The Seven Valleys, Bahá'u'lláh affirms the validity of the euphoria and joy brought by love, and He never seems to challenge romanticism in as direct a manner as He does ideologization and legalism. However, He strongly relativizes the euphoric element, making it only an early stage in the process of attaining authenticity (The Valley of Love), and He does explicitly identify one of the Sufi excesses, namely their particular view that the individual human self can ultimately fuse with or be absorbed into the divine essence. Indeed, Bahá'u'lláh characterizes the exponents of this quasipantheistic view as those who have declared themselves partners with God.[22]

It would thus seem that religious or mystic romanticism tends towards an unacceptable blurring of the legitimate boundaries of the self, leading perhaps either to manic self-exaltation or to an unhealthy preoccupation with oneself to the exclusion of others. One mistakes the self's absorption in itself for union with God. Bahá'u'lláh alludes to the nonauthentic character of this condition of spiritual self-absorption in such passages as the following:

> They that are the worshipers of the idol which their imaginations have carved, and who call it Inner Reality, such men are in truth accounted among the heathen.[23]

> And among the people is he who layeth claim to inner knowledge, and still deeper knowledge concealed within this knowledge. Say: Thou speakest false! By God! What thou dost possess is naught but husks which We have left to thee as bones are left to dogs.[24]

---

22. See the many references to this notion in, for example, Bahá'u'lláh, *Gleanings*.
23. Bahá'u'lláh, *Gleanings*, p. 338.
24. Bahá'u'lláh, *Kitáb-i-Aqdas*, para. no. 36.

In any case, those who have experienced the pangs and throes of romantic love know that it indeed "burneth to ashes the harvest of reason"[25] and destroys or limits one's ability to function authentically.

We thus see that each of the three fundamental human capacities of mind, will, and heart can give rise, if isolated from the others and taken to an extreme, to a distortion that is destructive of authenticity. Ideology, legalism, and romanticism show us that even God-given, spiritual capacities can be misused in a sincere attempt to achieve the capacity for relational authenticity. This should lead us to realize just how subtle the process of true moral development can be.

7. Humanisms and Non-Religious Ideologies

Besides the religiously based moralities, there are non-religious or areligious moralities that attempt to elaborate a coherent moral system without reference to intrinsic and universal values. Such systems may well be humanistic in the narrow sense that they give supreme value to one or another aspect of the human being, but they are inauthentic in that they provide no basis for distinguishing that which is universal and essential in human nature from what is purely local and accidental. Examples of such inauthentic humanisms are theories of racial superiority, which hold that the particular characteristics of some racial group are supreme over other human values; or various forms of militarism, which hold that the physically powerful have a natural right to dominate the weak.

Indeed, agnostic or atheistic humanisms may well hold that the human being is the highest value in existence (not just in creation, since God's existence is now discounted), but yet lack the notion of a universal intrinsic value inherent in the very being (essence) of each individual human. For example, *collectivism* is a humanism which holds that all human value resides in the collectivity: the individual

---

25. Bahá'u'lláh, *The Seven Valleys and The Four Valleys*, p. 8.

derives all of his value from society and the role he plays in the social context. From a purely collectivist viewpoint the individual,
considered in isolation from society, is literally without value (because now there is no notion of intrinsic value). Nor is collectivist
value universal, since it is usually defined with reference to some
particular collectivity. Non-ideologized communism, and its vari-
ants, represent a collectivist humanism, in which "the proletariat"
or "the people" play essentially the same role as does God for authentic religion.

Yet another humanist morality is *individualism*, which holds that
an individual may have value, but only insofar as he has demonstrated some special abilities or competency above the socially perceived norm or average. Individualistic value is thus particular to
each person. It is also extrinsic because it is defined with respect to
the norms of the given society. Hence, it is neither universal nor
intrinsic.

Thus, authentic morality is based on what is universal and intrinsic in essential human nature. If we negate intrinsicality, we get
systems like collectivism where all value is extrinsic to the individual.
If we negate universality, then we get a system such as individualism,
which gives value only or primarily to certain particular characteristics possessed by some individuals, but not shared by all humans.

Besides the humanistic moralities, there are also those based on
various non-religious, social, or political ideologies. We will not engage a detailed discussion of such moralities here, especially as we
have already treated thoroughly the case of religious ideologies (see
section 3, p. 8 ff.). Suffice it to say that social or political ideologies
share with religious ideologies the defect of exalting some doctrine
or principle above the human being and thus of giving moral justification to the sacrifice of humans or authentic human relations for
the propagation of the ideology.

However, the defects of purely humanistic moralities, such as
collectivism and individualism, are perhaps more subtle than the
defects of ideological moralities. We therefore devote the next two
sections to a closer examination of them.

8. Collectivism; the Pursuit of Power

We must each conceive of ourselves as having value, for to consider oneself worthless is to perpetrate spiritual or psychological suicide. Imagine that we belong to a society where all accept the collectivist notion that the only possible source of our individual value is what may be attributed to us by the society. In such a case, we have no choice but to seek our value from society. All of our social interactions will be affected by this universal pursuit of self-value attribution.

How will we carry forward this pursuit of personal value? Primarily by seeking power and dominance over others. We will seek out those positions (roles) in society which give us high status, power, and authority.

The logic is this: power and authority allow us to compel others to recognize our worth—to attribute value to us. Such power is exercised over others by the promise of reward and the threat of punishment or withholding of rewards, and it is acquired by occupying a role to which, however irrationally, society has attributed the requisite authority.

Social roles are like so many slots or pigeon holes, each with a value attached to it. Thus, when we occupy a position of high social status, we not only acquire the power and authority that characterizes the role, but we also have the illusion that the social value symbolically attributed to the role augments our own personal value. Thus, the pursuit of power is the underlying motif of human interactions in a collectivist society.

The nature of powerseeking is that it creates asymmetrical relationships between people. I cannot have power and dominance over you at the same time and in the same way that you have power and dominance over me. This asymmetry in turn leads to relational conflict. If you and I are each seeking power over the other in our interactions, then fundamentally we will be striving against each other, for we will each realize (perhaps instinctively or unconsciously) that only one of us can be successful. In the power game there are winners and losers, and this means that somebody will be unhappy in most every interaction, because the loser's feelings of oppression and domination are experienced negatively by all human beings. Moreover no one will be a winner in all situations, and winning itself is no protection against unhappiness: the consistent winner will be subject to increasing fear at the anticipation of possible future losses, and he will become the object of envy, jealousy, and periodic sabotage attempts on the part of others.

Hence, the relational asymmetry created by powerseeking is the very antithesis of the relational authenticity which is the proper goal of true moral striving. The mark of authentic relationships is altruistic love, which leads to reciprocity, mutuality, and symmetry, not to asymmetry and dominance. Moreover, in a relationship based on authentic love, both parties experience positive feelings, for it is the nature of love that it benefits both giver and receiver. Love is the prototypical "win-win" relationship in which everyone is happy.

Thus, the pursuit of authenticity and love leads to enduring happiness, whereas the pursuit of power is literally the pursuit of our own unhappiness. Yet, if we accept, albeit unconsciously, the collectivist notion of value, then we have no choice but to seek our value through the acquisition of power and status in society, because the only alternative is (so we think) the nonbeing of worthlessness, which no one can accept.

It is a fundamental truth of human nature that our actions and motivations are determined not by reality but by our perception of reality. Thus, even though it is objectively true that God exists, that He has created each of us, and that we each have an inalienable intrinsic value, if we are unaware of these truths then we will nevertheless act as if we do not have intrinsic value. This clearly illustrates the moral centrality of God and the need for a conscious authentic relationship with Him, for it is only through this relationship that we gain an awareness and an understanding of our intrinsic value. It is this knowledge and awareness alone that enable us to avoid such purely humanistic value conceptions as collectivism and to develop the inner strength necessary to renounce the pursuit of power.

In more general terms, we pursue power because we feel weak and vulnerable, and we think (perceive) that an accretion of power will make us strong and invulnerable. We consider ourselves weak because of what we do not possess and we see power as the means to acquisition and possession. But the objective reality is that possession is an illusion. We possess nothing; all is in the hands of God and utterly under His control and power. He alone gives or with-holds, and He has already given us our intrinsic value in the form of our immortal and inalienable spiritual capacities of consciousness, mind, heart, and will. Once we know this fully, the illusion of pos-session is destroyed forever and the impulse to seek power recedes within us. We are freed from the tyranny of the power imperative. We are free to be happy.

Our brief examination of collectivism has thus allowed us to identify at least one positive principle of authentic moral striving: *replacing the pursuit of power by the pursuit of love.* The resistance we all feel to renouncing the pursuit of power is a measure of how far humanity has strayed from authentic morality. Indeed, correcting this fundamental error is one of the main purposes of Bahá'u'lláh's revelation:

> And amongst the realms of unity is the unity of rank and station. It redoundeth to the exaltation of the Cause, glorifying it among all peoples. Ever since the seeking of preference and distinction came into play, the world hath been laid waste. It hath become desolate. Those who have quaffed from the ocean of divine utterance and fixed their gaze upon the Realm of Glory should regard themselves as being on the same level as the oth-ers and in the same station. Were this matter to be definitely established and conclusively demonstrated through the power and might of God, the world would become as the Abhá Para-dise.
>
> Indeed, man is noble, inasmuch as each one is a repository of the sign of God. Nevertheless, to regard oneself as superior in knowledge, learning or virtue, or to exalt oneself or seek pref-erence, is a grievous transgression. Great is the blessedness of those who are adorned with the ornament of this unity and have been graciously confirmed by God.[26]

---

26. Bahá'u'lláh, quoted in *Messages from the Universal House of Justice: 1963–1986*, no. 206:3a–b.

Let us stress here the important point that renouncing the pursuit of power does not mean abolishing social roles, but rather changing the way we look at social roles. Any viable society must have differentiated roles and functions; it cannot and does not exist simply as a collection of individuals. Indeed, Bahá'u'lláh has Himself spoken of the necessity of preserving the integrity of "every rank and station."[27] But differentiation of function does not in itself necessitate differentiation of personal value or a lack of reciprocity in personal relationships.

If I am a sick airline pilot who visits you in your capacity as a doctor, there is no necessary presumption that you are better than I because I am momentarily dependent on your professional competency. We are free to relate as equally valuable individuals who respect each other's differentiated functions in society. But if we live in a society which considers doctors, say, to be of higher status than airline pilots, and if we consider that we have no value as human beings beyond what is given us by the society, then you will cling to your superior value relative to mine, and this will change completely the nature of our interaction, producing a fundamental asymmetry in the relationship. Your attempts to restore my health will not be primarily for my sake as a valuable human being. Rather, such efforts as you deploy will become self-indulgent demonstrations of your professional competency and a celebration of your power over me, of my helplessness, and of my dependency on you. The widespread perception that such asymmetries are inevitable derives primarily from the general unawareness of intrinsic value in today's societies.

It is perhaps surprising to realize that a morality such as collectivism, which after all gives value to the human, can be so antihuman in its consequences and create such widespread unhappiness. But this shows just how important a true religious foundation is for authentic morality. Indeed, a superhuman God or Creator is the only logically possible source of a universal human nature—a universal intrinsic value inherent in the very being (essence) of each individual human.

---

27. Bahá'u'lláh, *Gleanings*, p. 188.

Collectivism is not the only destructive humanism, as our analysis of its polar opposite, individualism, will show.

9. Individualism and Competition

Recall that individualism gives value to personal ability that is demonstrably above the perceived norm in society. Individualism is the supervaluation of the special. In a society where all accept the individualistic notion of value, we can avoid the self-perception of worthlessness only by demonstrating special ability in some way. This is done primarily through *competition*, i.e. by constantly striving to outperform others and thereby to demonstrate our superior ability in a given area of endeavor. Each time we "win" a competition by demonstrably outperforming another, we (and others) perceive an increase in our personal value.

In other words, since individualism lacks the notion of intrinsic value it impels us to seek our value through competition just as collectivism incites us to seek our value through power and dominance. Just as powerseeking is the underlying motif of collectivism, so competition is the underlying motif of individualism. Moreover, the two motifs are not exclusive. In a sufficiently unspiritual society we can have the worst of both worlds: powerseeking and competition.

Competition proceeds by a horizontal comparison of the performance of two different individuals at the same time. If we seek to determine whether you or I are better at playing the violin, then we will each play before a similar audience at approximately the same time, and the comparison between our two performances will be the basis of a social judgment as to which of us is superior.

The logic of competition is, in some ways, similar to the logic of powerseeking (though there are important differences as well). I cannot outperform you at the same time and in the same way that you can outperform me. Thus, like powerseeking, competition leads to asymmetrical relationships and hence to relational conflict. However, winning a competition in a given area of endeavor does not necessarily confer any direct power or dominance of winner over loser. But in an individualistic society it does result in the attribution of a higher personal value to the winner than to the loser. This value differential means that losers will have a deflated and negative self-image (at least to the extent that they are unaware of their intrinsic value).

Thus when competition becomes the dominant mode of interaction in a society, relational authenticity and hence authentic morality are defeated. Individual members of the society become prey to immense stress. People feel alienated and alone, and they find it difficult to trust others and to communicate effectively with them.

If we live in such a society, we will tend to perceive ourselves as weak and vulnerable, and will be often haunted by the fear that others may discover our weaknesses and use this knowledge against us. We will thus attempt to project an image of strength to others and to hide self-perceived weaknesses. This creates further alienation, hypocrisy, and ultimately self-deception as we strive to hide our weaknesses not only from others but from ourselves as well.

In highly individualistic societies where competitive modes of interaction are prevalent (e.g., North America or Western Europe) the negative impact of competition on human relationships has been generally recognized and acknowledged, at least in recent years. Nevertheless, social philosophers continue to purvey the notion that competition is necessary to the pursuit of excellence. We are told that the stress, tension, and unhappiness resulting from life in an environment of continual competition are the price we must pay for excellence. Comparisons are frequently drawn between the (supposedly high) level of development in individualistic societies and the (presumably lower) level of achievement in less competitive societies. This perceived difference in development is held to demonstrate conclusively that competition is productive of and necessary to excellence.

In this way, the identification of the pursuit of excellence with competition has become gradually and uncritically accepted as an established fact. That this identification is false can be readily seen by a thoughtful analysis of what is involved in each of these endeavors.

On one hand, the pursuit of excellence can be viewed as the vertical comparison of two different performances by the same person at two different times. If tomorrow I can play the violin better than I can today, then that is progress towards excellence. Whether, at any point in this vertical pursuit, I can play better than you is beside the point entirely. If I have great native ability, it may be that I can easily outperform you without my making any real progress towards personal perfection.

On the other hand, competition is the lateral comparison between the performance of two different people at the same time. Thus, the vertical pursuit of excellence is orthogonal to the lateral pursuit of competition: the two endeavors are fundamentally different.

Of course it is possible that competitive comparison between two performances can stimulate each performer to pursue excellence, but this happens *only* when excellence is the conscious goal of each. Let us examine this in more detail.

Suppose I am striving to outperform you. What strategies can I deploy to achieve this goal? One strategy is to improve my performance over time (pursue excellence) so that I can eventually outperform you. But what if you are also striving to improve your performance? No matter how much progress I make, I have no guarantee that you will not make equal or greater progress and that I will never be successful in outperforming you.

Of course, if excellence is our goal, then there is no problem. The world will be better off with two excellent performers instead of two mediocre performers where one is recognizably better than the other. But if winning the mutual competition is my goal, then I will not be content with striving for excellence year after year only to see you continue to outperform me (because your performance is also improving).

Thus, the pursuit of excellence is not the optimal strategy for winning a competition. What better strategy is there? The answer is: *sabotage*. Sabotaging your opponent's performance (and preventing him or her from sabotaging your own) will be a superior strategy for winning the competition. It takes much less energy than the pursuit of excellence and the outcome is quicker and surer.

We can now understand clearly the fundamental difference between competition and the pursuit of excellence. On the one hand, sabotage is always a reasonable strategy and often the preferred strategy for winning a competition. On the other hand, sabotage can never, under any circumstances, lead to an increase in excellence on the part of either the saboteur or the sabotee.

Because it is a vertical pursuit, the quest for excellence elevates us to a higher plane. It is part of the pursuit of God and Godliness as the ultimate value, for God is always above and beyond us. But the lateral striving of competition leads us to work against others not with them. It wastes energy we can apply to pursuing excellence, and it distracts us from the source of excellence—the intrinsic value of our God-given capacities of mind, heart, and will—by focusing our attention on the weaknesses and vulnerabilities of others.

The moral difference between competition and the pursuit of excellence lies principally in our motivation. Pursuing excellence is a form of worshiping God as the ultimate value, whereas the motive for striving to outperform others is most often a form of pride. Yet, the act itself (performing at a certain level) may be the same in both cases!

This illustrates another important principle of authentic morality: it is only in relationship to the underlying motive that any physical action can be morally evaluated. Physical acts taken in isolation from their context do not have an intrinsic moral value. This principle is universal, as 'Abdu'l-Bahá clearly affirms in the following passage:

> O thou son of the Kingdom! All things are beneficial if joined with the love of God; and without His love all things are harmful, and act as a veil between man and the Lord of the Kingdom. . . . every branch of learning, conjoined with the love of God, is approved and worthy of praise; but bereft of His love, learning is barren—indeed, it bringeth on madness. Every kind of knowledge, every science, is as a tree: if the fruit of it be

the love of God, then is it a blessed tree, but if not, that tree is but dried-up wood, and shall only feed the fire.[28]

This passage from 'Abdu'l-Bahá also serves to remind us once again that the roots of authentic morality lie within the recesses of our hearts, where our acts are conceived, and cannot be measured by external conformity to ethical rules alone.

In passing, a word should be said regarding the several passages from the Bahá'í writings in which believers are urged to "vie with one another" in the path of God, thus (by implication) to "compete spiritually" with each other. Some may feel that these passages validate the moral authenticity of competition, thus contradicting the strong contention that competition is spiritually inauthentic. The answer is that the competition being urged in the Bahá'í writings is a competition of service towards others, not a competition of dominance or superiority. This is clear when, for example, 'Abdu'l-Bahá says "Happy the soul that shall forget his own good, and like the chosen ones of God, vie with his fellows in service to the good of all . . ."[29]

If I succeed in serving you more than you serve me, it will hardly cause depressed self-esteem on your part. This is entirely different from the competition we have discussed above, which is a striving *against* others not *towards* them in service. Whenever we need to clarify in our minds the difference between the two forms of competition, we need only recall our initial definition of competition: striving to outperform the other with the goal of attributing to oneself a higher personal value than the other.

Striving towards excellence for the love of God is not only a morally superior motive to competitive striving, but also more difficult to achieve, requiring as it does a considerably higher level of moral maturity. In the short run, it is much easier to incite motivation by competition than by the pure pursuit of excellence, and this is undoubtedly one of the reasons why the identification of the two

---

28. 'Abdu'l-Bahá, *Selections from the Writings of 'Abdu'l-Bahá*, no. 154:3.
29. 'Abdu'l-Bahá, *The Secret of Divine Civilization*, p. 116.

pursuits has become so generally accepted as an established fact. Indeed, learning how to pursue excellence, without giving in to jealousy towards others or yielding to the temptation to sabotage them, is one of the challenges of authentic morality.

10. Social Norms, Material Values, and Spiritual Values

Prevalent competition is not the only negative consequence of an individualistic social milieu. Individualism's supervaluation of the special leads to a general devaluation of whatever is perceived as normal or ordinary. Indeed, in a highly individualistic society the worst insult that can be proffered to an individual is to say he is "ordinary," because this means he has no special ability and thus no (individualistic) value.

Consider, for example, the individualistic societies of North America and Western Europe, which give extremely high value to successful athletes and cinema actors, who are paid enormous sums of money to display their particular abilities and talents. Contrast this with the generally low value these same societies give to motherhood, which is devalued because it is "ordinary": supposedly "anyone" can be a mother; it takes no special ability.

However, when viewed from the spiritual perspective of authentic morality, motherhood is the primary and most valuable role in society. Indeed, we can observe that even "ordinary" mothers give priority to the needs of their children over their own needs at virtually every instant from the birth of a child until it becomes an autonomous adult. Not only is this "common" degree of self-sacrifice an extraordinary phenomenon, it is the very foundation of society: if only one generation of women refused to play this role it would be the end of the human race. Yet, our individualistic Western societies take the self-sacrifice of mothers for granted while laying immense social energy and resources at the feet of professional athletes and rock musicians, who perform no vital social function whatsoever. Indeed, the complete disappearance of these latter roles from society would be of little significance to the progress of humanity.

Moreover, as the case of mothers versus rock musicians shows, the very notion of what is "normal" or "ordinary" is extremely unclear. For example, let us imagine a society in which the capacities and achievements of a Beethoven or an Einstein were common currency: virtually everyone has the ability to write Beethoven's Symphony no. 9 or conceive of the theory of relativity. In such a society, these abilities and achievements would be ordinary and thus taken for granted. If, further, the society were based on an individualistic value system, these now "ordinary" abilities would be less valued than those (of whatever nature) perceived as special or above the norm.

Science has shown that, in any stable population with random mating (any two individuals of the opposite sex are equally likely to mate), talents and abilities are *normally distributed* according to the well-known Gaussian or bell-shaped curve. What this means practically is that, whatever the norm of a given collectivity may be, the vast majority (about 68%) of the population will be normal. Thus, in a society where only the supernormal is valued, at most ten or fifteen percent of the population has any hope of demonstrating superior ability at a level sufficient to be perceived as special by the population as a whole. Hence, an individualistic value system guarantees that the majority of people will be devalued (and thus unhappy), *no matter how high the actual level of achievement of the majority of individuals may be*. This mathematical analysis of normality is the ultimate *reductio ad absurdum* of individualism as a viable moral system.

In light of the above analysis, one can legitimately wonder how such a morally inauthentic value system could have become so widespread. Part of the answer undoubtedly lies in the confusion between competition and the pursuit of excellence that we have discussed above. However, another significant factor appears to have been a similar confusion between spiritual (intangible) and material (tangible) values.

According to virtually all modern theories of economy, material (economic) values are based primarily on the principle of rarity:

the greater the rarity of a material good, the greater its value. This leads, in turn, to what is held to be the fundamental principle governing human economic behavior, *competition for rarity*.

The logic of these principles derives from the fact that material values are diminished when they are shared. If I have an apple and must share it with you, then we will each have half an apple. Moreover, the greater the population that must share the apple (the rarer it is), the less each person's share will be and the greater the value attributed to the apple. Thus, there will be competition for possession of the apple and the control of its distribution (sharing).

The principle of competition for rarity seems to describe accurately quite a bit of economic behavior, though modern, high-tech means of production have begun to undermine this principle. (Which would you rather possess: a very good computer, which you need and is easily available for a few hundred dollars, or a precious stone potentially worth thousands of dollars but which is of absolutely no use to you?)

Be that as it may, the point is that this principle is totally false when applied to spiritual values because *spiritual values are multiplied and enhanced, not diminished, when shared*. If I have a good idea and share it with you, then we both have a good idea. The more the idea is shared the more valuable it becomes. Or, if I have love and share it with you, then you will most likely respond in a loving manner, because love evokes love. Thus, material values are diminished when shared whereas spiritual values are enhanced when shared.

Moreover, spiritual values (such as motherhood) are universal, whereas material values are local and limited. This means that the materialistic notion of normality simply does not apply to spiritual values. The more spiritual values are shared—the more "normal" or "ordinary" they become within a given society— the greater their worth. Thus, it is not competition but cooperation (sharing) which enhances spiritual values.

Of course, we can only share something we have in the first place, and this applies to spiritual values as well as material values. We are thus led back to the notion of intrinsic value: each of us is naturally endowed with a personal source of spiritual values in the form of our inherent capacities of mind, heart, and will. Hence the awareness of intrinsic value, when coupled with the clear knowledge of the universality of spiritual values, completely alters the traditional logic of competition for rarity, transforming it into a logic of cooperation for universality.

We can now understand that the basic logic of individualistic competition derives in large measure from an inappropriate application to the spiritual realm of certain principles that do have a genuine (if limited) validity in the material realm. We have thus confused the merely general or mediocre with the universal and valuable. The material realm and the spiritual realm each obey certain laws and principles, but spiritual laws are not in all cases the same as material laws. A confusion between the two can result in an inauthentic moral system.

11. Summary and Conclusion

We have seen that reality is structured as a value hierarchy, with God the supreme value and humanity the greatest created value. As the ultimate value in existence, God is the ultimate goal of all human moral striving. Since there can be no direct connection between the transcendent essence of God and any created entity, God has ordained and established a link (religia) between Himself and humanity through His Manifestations. When we respond appropriately to God's overtures to us (by recognizing the Manifestation and obeying His laws), then there is established an authentic relationship between ourselves and God, and this vertical relationship becomes the basis of establishing authentic lateral relationships between ourselves and other human beings. The development and enhancement of these authentic relationships constitutes, as ordained by God Himself, the pursuit of Divinity as the ultimate moral value.

Moral development is thus the pursuit of relational authenticity. This endeavor is carried forward primarily by the proper and balanced development, within ourselves and in others, of the intrinsic capacities of mind, heart, and will with which God has endowed each human soul. However, we have seen that it is very easy to mis-understand this process and to replace the pursuit of relational au-thenticity by certain morally inauthentic alternatives. Among these false alternatives are: ideology, which pursues the propagation of cer-tain doctrines that are held to be more important than authentic human relations; legalism, which considers that morality can be re-duced to some set of rules for ethical behavior; and romanticism, which considers the euphoric feelings of love as the ultimate goal of moral striving.

Even though the intrinsic value of our inherent capacities is part of the reality created by God, and thus exists objectively (i.e., independently of our perception of it), we may nevertheless fail to apprehend this value. Since our behavior is largely determined by our perception of reality rather than reality itself, we may act as if we do not have intrinsic value, seeking vainly to acquire value from others or from society through powerseeking, competition, and sabo-tage. Though such pursuits are the very antithesis of authenticity and inevitably lead to our unhappiness, we may nevertheless feel that these inauthentic pursuits are the only alternative to viewing ourselves as worthless and thus morally nonexistent.

It is only within the context of an authentic relationship with God that we become fully cognizant of our intrinsic value, and this knowledge alone gives us the courage to pursue authentic relation-ships and to resist the lure of inauthentic alternatives. The tempta-tion for inauthenticity derives from the fact that these alternatives are easier to pursue (at least in the short run), promising as they do an immediate gratification. It is much easier for me to believe in a set of doctrines or follow a set of rules (and to perceive myself as su-perior to others for doing so) than to serve others in loving humility.

Establishing and maintaining an authentic relationship with God is thus the key to all authentic relationships. As our discussion in the ensuing chapters will show, this is an ongoing, dynamic pro-cess, not a static condition that is achieved once and for all.

Chapter 2

The Process of
Moral Development

1. Introduction: Autonomy and
Spiritual Well-Being

The initial configuration of each human life is one in which the fundamental capacities of the soul are a pure, unactualized potential. According to the Bahá'í Writings, this potential is inherent in the soul, inalienable from the soul, and eternally fixed (it cannot be either increased or decreased). Thus, we know the soul's potential has ultimate limits, but we do not know what these limits are, and the Bahá'í Writings tell us that the fundamental purpose of our existence is the development of this potential in both ourselves and others.[1]

---

1. The exposition of this chapter builds upon a number of the author's previously published works, but principally "The Concept of Spirituality," first published in the monograph series *Bahá'í Studies*, Vol. 11, and "The Kitáb-i-Aqdas: The Causality Principle in the World of Being," first published in *The Bahá'í World: 1993–94*, pp. 189–236. However, both of these essays have now been published in whole in *The Law of Love Enshrined*, pp. 189–249 and pp. 113–157, respectively. Since each of these previous articles contains copious citations from the Bahá'í Writings—and virtually all of those to which we would refer for the exposition of chapter 2—we will cite the appropriate passages and sections from *The*

Beginning with this initial configuration, the life of each individual consists of the gradual unfoldment or actualization of his intrinsic potential by means of progressively richer (and more complex) interactions with his environment. The Bahá'í Writings tell us that three of the most fundamental capacities of the soul are the understanding capacity or mind, the feeling capacity, or heart, and the desiring/acting capacity, or will. The immediate products of these capacities are ideas, feelings and emotions, and desires (intentions) and actions. The ultimate products of these capacities, *subsequent to appropriate interactions with the environment,* are knowledge (= true ideas), love (= positive and authentic feelings), and service (= right actions).[2]

The process of spiritual development, or spiritual education, is learning how to generate and sustain appropriate interactions with our environment. This process has two aspects: (1) developing our inner resources to respond appropriately to unexpected events or to actions by the environment on us, and (2) learning how to initiate positive and productive interactions with the environment. It is in this authentic dialogue between ourselves and the various phenomena (aspects) of reality that we develop our intrinsic capacities.

The ultimate goal of spiritual education is to produce a genuinely happy and authentically autonomous human being. It is this combination of autonomy (self-development) and well-being (authentic happiness) which alone enables us to sustain authentic relationships with God, ourselves, and others, and thus to achieve the true goal of moral development. Previous systems of morality have tended to put the emphasis exclusively or principally on happiness, neglecting the importance of autonomy. This neglect has had several unfortunate consequences.

In the first place, autonomy is the more fundamental of the two pillars of spiritual education. Genuine well-being results primarily

---

Law of Love Enrshrined in preference to direct references to the original sources. It is hoped and intended that this practice will abridge and simplify the exposition of chapter 2. With reference to the concepts and notions mentioned in the first paragraph of the present essay, see *The Law of Love Enshrined,* pp. 118–121; 193–202.

2. See *The Law of Love Enshrined,* pp. 222–228.

from the achievement of autonomy: happiness cannot be success-fully pursued for its own sake alone, in isolation from autonomy. As 'Abdu'l-Bahá has said: ". . . human happiness is founded upon spiri-tual behavior."[3]

Indeed it is precisely the attempt to pursue happiness without the discipline of autonomous development that has led to the vari-ous inauthentic moral pursuits discussed in chapter 1, such as ideol-ogy, legalism, or romanticism. We must know, at every stage of our development process, that true and enduring happiness results only from genuine moral autonomy. The basis of this knowledge is aware-ness of our intrinsic value, as discussed in chapter 1.

If we do not maintain a continual awareness of our intrinsic value and God-given potential, we will find it difficult to generate the courage necessary to sacrifice a lesser and ephemeral happiness in the short run for the achievement of an increase in autonomy and thus of a long-term authentic happiness. Yet it is precisely such choices that we must make over and over again as we pursue authentic moral development.

Indeed, we discover that, with each new stage of autonomy, there corresponds an appropriate level of well-being and happiness. The more we are committed to the pursuit of self-development and further autonomy, rather than being satisfied with the pleasant sen-sations of happiness related to certain achievements, the swifter will be our growth and our transition to a yet higher stage of autonomy and its corresponding greater degree of spiritual well-being.

At every stage of our development, we interact with the world on the basis of whatever perception of reality we have then attained. This inner perception, or *inner model*, of reality is the key to under-standing the dynamics of human behaviour. This model will gener-ally be a mosaic incorporating both true and false perceptions into a seamless whole. The gradual purification of our inner model of its false elements (often called "vain imaginings" in the Bahá'í Writ-ings) is a necessary part of the process of optimizing our autonomy

---

3. 'Abdu'l-Bahá, *Selections from the Writings of 'Abdu'l-Bahá*, no. 100:2.

and well-being. In this chapter we will examine the fundamental elements involved in the process of actualizing our intrinsic potential and purifying our inner model.

2. Developing Curricula for Youth and Young Adults

In the beginning of this life/education process, one is more reactive and acted upon than proactive. Thus, the spiritual education of children is a process that, for better or worse, is largely in the hands of those who instruct them, be they parents, family members, or teachers. However, an individual participates more deliberately and actively in the process as his or her soul's potential is progressively actualized. This means that there must be a significant difference between curricula designed for the moral and spiritual education of youth (post-puberty) and young adults and those designed for children.

Speaking in general terms, children are spontaneously happy (because of their innocence and ignorance of evil) but not autonomous. Young adults are relatively autonomous, if they have undergone anything like normal development, but are genuinely happy only if their capacities have been *properly* developed. We will examine further on just what such a "proper" development may mean, but for the moment the important point is that, in today's world, extremely few individuals are fortunate enough to have had access to an educational experience that allows them to achieve proper development.

The result is the pattern we see in today's youth all over the world: they have the freedom and capacity to choose, but are basically unhappy and do not know how to make productive use of their freedom. Thus, they turn towards various substitutes for genuine happiness: sexual promiscuity; drugs, alcohol, and other substances that act on the central nervous system; gross material acquisition; pursuit of power and status within a social group; violence; raucous and shocking music; and other such techniques for generating temporary but intense emotional sensations.

Curricula for the moral and spiritual education of youth and young adults must, if they are to be successful, address this basic, existing configuration. Such curricula must take into account the fact that the student is an autonomous adult whose behavior, ideas, and attitudes will change when and only when he or she consciously decides (on the basis of an intrinsic motivation) to change them.

In teaching children, adult authorities can count on the fact that their students are natural imitators who seek and want their approval. Adult teachers can therefore instill in children certain attitudes, ideas, and actions whose validity the students can test as they grow towards adult autonomy. But, youth and young adults have little if any need for the approval of adults. Moreover, not only do they *not* seek to imitate their elders (whom they largely regard as hypocritical in the first place), their autonomy and growing sense of independence makes them naturally inclined to resist and rebel against whatever comes from adult authority.

Thus, any successful curriculum of moral education for youth in today's world must talk to them as equals, recognize and validate their experience of the world—the pain, hypocrisy, and evil it contains—and facilitate their acquisition of the intrinsic motivation to make those moral choices and generate those spiritual responses that will lead them from the valley of moral misery to the summits of spiritual well-being. And we must help them discover the spiritual passion and excitement involved in this process, for therein lies the source of a truly intrinsic motivation, rather than a sporadic motivation generated by outside pressures or periodic life crises.

In the development of such a curriculum, the fundamental task is to understand the basic dynamics of *value choice*—the mechanism by which any individual comes to perceive something as valuable and to base his actions on that perception. Such an understanding can only come from a true and accurate conception of the spiritual and material nature of the human being. The sources for an accurate concept of the human reality are, on the one hand, religion—more particularly at this critical period of history the Bahá'í Faith and its Writings—and, on the other hand, science—logical concepts tested and refined by experience and experiments.

Thus, our goal is to develop a scientifically based, Bahá'í-inspired curriculum for youth and young adults. Scientific ideas or theories may be said to be "Bahá'í-inspired" if they have been carefully weighed in the balance of the Writings of the Bahá'í Faith and integrated into the basic spiritual conception (paradigm) of the human being given by Bahá'u'lláh. Since the unity of religion and science is one of the basic Bahá'í teachings, the task we undertake is thus both thoroughly scientific and thoroughly Bahá'í.[4]

3. Interactions—the Basic Unit of Human Experience

There can be no doubt that, from the moment of conception, the individual's interaction with his environment is continual and uninterrupted. Life is the persistence of being and the flow of experience. Moreover, there is a potentially infinite diversity of environments with which each individual can interact. Indeed, since no two people occupy the same position within a given environment, it is accurate to say that no two people develop within identical environments.

In the light of the dynamics and richness of human experience, one could thus legitimately wonder whether there are any truly universal principles underlying the process of spiritual development. The Bahá'í Writings affirm that such principles do exist, primarily because of two fundamental features of reality: (1) The ways in which human beings are similar are greater and more fundamental than the ways they are different; and (2) although the number of *entities* within our environment may be potentially infinite, there are only a

---

4. In "The Tablet of the Universe," 'Abdu'l-Bahá speaks of the dual and complementary application of science and revelation in the following terms: "Know then that those mathematical questions which have stood the test of scrutiny and about the soundness of which there is no doubt are those that are supported by incontrovertible and logically binding proofs and by the rules of geometry as applied to astronomy, that are based on observations of the stars and careful astronomical research, and are also in conformity with the principles of the universal themes expounded in the divine sciences." (See provisional, unpublished English translation, Haifa, 1995, p. 7.)

finite number of *categories of entities* to which we must learn to relate properly. The principles involved in relating to each category are universal and can be explicitly learned. Individual differences arise only in particular interactions, and these provide a welcome diversity and creativity to our life. They also prevent life from being a mere formula or algorithm that we can blindly and uniformly apply to each situation. In other words, universal principles can be learned ahead of time, but the application and implementation of these principles is never wholly predictable and always requires some creative effort on our part.[5]

Since our lives are clearly the sum of all our experiences and our reactions to these experiences, individual life can be reasonably viewed as the collection of all interactions between the individual and reality. To provide a solid theoretical foundation for our approach, we therefore posit the existence of discrete *interactions* as the basic and irreducible unit of human life experience. We assume that any such interaction involves some change in the inner states of the individual. In the light of these hypotheses, individual life is definable as a series of interactions between the individual and various portions of reality and thus as a series of discrete changes in the inner states of the individual.

So defined, interactions are ideal entities which, in our theory, play a role similar to that of the genes of biology, the elementary particles of quantum mechanics, or the "capabilities" of the educational theorist Farzam Arbab. In order to proceed with our development, it is not necessary to answer the philosophical question of whether or not interactions have objective existence. The assumption of their existence is a typical simplifying assumption of science, enabling us to construct a reasonably accurate model of the process of human spiritual growth and development. If a more useful theoretical framework eventually emerges from our work, then it should not be difficult to translate from the present theory into the more useful one.

---

5. *The Law of Love Enshrined*, pp. 134–157; 232–249.

However, it is perhaps worthwhile to note that recent research on the mechanism by which the human brain treats the raw data of physical perception has established that this process is chronologically discrete. The data itself is not physically localized but is rather stored in fragments over the whole of the cerebral cortex. These fragments are then instantiated into a total image when the separate neurons are fired in a synchronized manner by a wave of nerve impulses, emitted by the thalamus, that sweep over the cortex at regular intervals. Thus, physical perception appears to be a series of *clichés*, or still images, which, because they occur frequently and at regular intervals, give the illusion of continuous perception.

These results are clearly interesting and relevant to our assumptions, but it is important to realize that our hypothesis of the existence of discrete interactions applies to all experience (including, for example, the inner perception of emotional states or of ideas) and not just to perceptions by the external sense organs. Again, we stress that this is an assumption we deliberately make in order to simplify our theory.[6]

We now turn to the task of categorizing the basic interactions of the individual.

4. The Fundamental Interactions of the Self

In all that follows, we will use the word "self" to refer to the soul (sometimes called the "spirit") of the individual as defined in the Bahá'í Writings. The basic interactions of the self are categorized as follows:

1. Self with the Divine (higher subjectivity). [D]
    Thus, Divine = God or Manifestations. [G,M]

---

6. The assumption that interactions are discrete is probably true for interactions involving material reality in some way, but most likely false once the physical body is no longer involved (ie., after physical death). However, it is clearly part of God's purpose that we begin our eternal spiritual journey as material/spiritual hybrids, subject to material limitations. Since our model of the spiritual growth process seeks to picture as accurately as possible the conditions of our present, earthly life, the assumption of discreteness seems eminently justified, even if our ultimate spiritual environment is or will be one of continuous interactions.

2. Self with the self. [S]
3. Self with another human subject. [H]
4. Self with objects. Objects may be concrete (perceptible by physical senses) or abstract (not concrete). Concrete objects may be animate or inanimate. [Ob, Ab, Ct, An, In]
5. Self with systems (collections) of objects. [COb]
6. Self with social groups (collections of human subjects). [CH]
7. Self with mixed environment (objects and subjects). [C]

Fig. 2.1. Basic interactions of the self

We symbolize these and exhibit their relationships as follows:

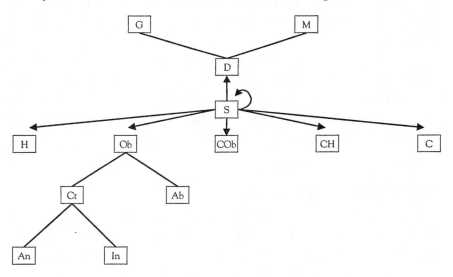

Key to the Diagram:

G = God
D = Divine
H = Human(s)
Ct = Concrete Objects
An = Animate concrete objects
COb = Systems or collections of objects
C = Mixed environment (objects and subjects)

M = Manifestations
S = Self
Ob = Objects
Ab = Abstract Objects
In = Inanimate concrete objects
CH = Collections of human subjects

Fig. 2.2. Diagram of the basic interactions of the self

Since all interactions are defined from the point of view of the individual soul, we classify a given interaction by the category of entities involved in that interaction.

It is clear that the last category of interaction—between the self and a system composed of subjects and objects—is somewhat of a catch-all, and one could argue that all interactions are multifaceted. For example, one could reasonably hold that every interaction is at least partly an interaction of the self with the self. Again, rather than engaging in a sterile debate as to whether or not "pure" interactions of each type truly exist, we relativize the whole scheme by categorizing interactions according to the clearly *dominant* element involved in a given interaction. Thus, a category 7 interaction is one in which no object or subject of the system is dominant; or a category 6 interaction is one in which no individual human subject is dominant, etc.

Once we will have examined the basic capacities of the self, we will proceed to examine those principles that are true of all interactions and those that are specific to a certain category of interactions. But first we must turn to a consideration of the capacities of the self in relation to interactions.

5. Capacities of the Self

There can be no doubt that consciousness or self-awareness is the most fundamental characteristic and defining capacity of the human being. Because we have consciousness, we have a *subjectivity*, i.e., a world of inner, subjective states to which only we have direct (unmediated) access. The existence of this inner world makes of each human being a *subject* and not just an object or a machine.

We experience our subjectivity as a constant flow of inner experience of various degrees of richness. We are continually filled with ideas, thoughts, concepts, feelings, perceptions, or sensations. Some of these inner data appear to be directly linked to phenomena that are *objective*, i.e., wholly outside the inner states of any human being; whereas other inner sensations are experienced as either self-generated or else generated by certain exchanges with other subjects like ourselves. In any case, every interaction between an individual and reality takes place by impinging upon or influencing the flow of internal experiences and sensations. Thus, the inner world of our subjectivity is truly the "universe" in which we live. This, as we shall see, is part of the purpose of God, for this inner world is the only environment over which we have a significant degree of control. If we pollute this inner space, it is we who will suffer the consequences, for it is we who live in that world.

Some would doubtless contend that animals may or do also have consciousness. The evidence for such an assertion is questionable at best, but, once again, we do not have to resolve this issue to proceed. Whatever limited analog of human consciousness may exist among animals is of such a different nature from human consciousness as to constitute a distinct category of existence, that of animate objects. Thus, following the Bahá'í Writings, we will assume that the realms of conscious existence are limited to humans, the Manifestations, and to God Himself. These three are the only categories of consciousness that exist, according to the Bahá'í Writings.[7]

The Bahá'í Writings explain that the first and highest specific capacity that God has given to humanity is the capacity of mind or understanding. This capacity is quite flexible, but one can identify at least the following more specific abilities of the mind:

Experience or perception:
- the ability to reflect or mirror an outer reality by a corresponding inner state

Intuition or synthesis:
- the ability to conceive of an entity or system in its totality, not just as a juxtaposition of its parts

Logic or analysis:
- the ability to proceed from the global perception of a configuration to a study of its parts and the relationship of the parts to each other[8]

7. See *The Law of Love Enshrined*, pp. 114–115; 121–124.
8. See *The Law of Love Enshrined*, p. 222–228.

The second main capacity of the human soul is the heart or affective capacity. This capacity allows us to experience feelings and emotions, and most particularly the emotion of love, which is a feeling of attraction towards some entity deriving from the sense that this entity is valuable. (Thus, love is our natural response to the perception of value.) More generally, every pure emotion is experienced as either positive and pleasant or else negative and unpleasant. This binary quality of feelings is, as we shall see, the ultimate basis of values and value choices.[9]

Of course, emotions may be complex and we may experience feelings with a mixture of pain and pleasure. However, we will assume that there do exist primary sensations of pure pain and of pure pleasure and that feelings which are ambiguous in tone are the result of a mixture of primary emotions some of which elicit pure pain and others pure pleasure. This, then, is another of our simplifying assumptions.

The third basic capacity of the human soul is the will, which endows us with the ability to initiate actions (interactions) and to sustain an action when once initiated. The will is also essential to the generation of desires, motivations, and intentions. Indeed, the most natural response to strong emotions is the desire to act in some way: when we are afraid we desire to run or to fight and when we love we are moved to approach the beloved object and establish a harmonious relationship with it. More generally, we spontaneously seek to repeat or reproduce those interactions which produce positive feelings and to flee or avoid those which produce negative emotions.[10]

However, if our goal in life is to increase our spiritual autonomy and well-being, we must learn to differentiate between interactions that produce initially pleasant feelings while being destructive in the long run (e.g., drug euphoria) and those that are ultimately productive but involve initial unpleasantness. Such a differentiation can only be based on accurate and adequate knowledge of spiritual

---

9. Ibid.
10. Ibid.

reality, a knowledge that enables us to defer immediate gratification in order to obtain a greater or more lasting benefit in the long run. (Thus, a student may experience the discipline of study as less pleasant than good times with his friends, but forego the latter in order to avoid the long term pain and frustration of being denied certain life opportunities that are dependent on the successful completion of his education.)

6. Actualizing the Self

The *person* or true self of the individual exists from the moment of its creation by God, but initially its capacities are a pure potential, as we have already observed. As these capacities are developed, this potential is actualized in the form of an increasingly rich *personality*. The soul is like a prism and the personality the particular spectrum of colors into which the prism refracts the white light of the pure human spirit. Some prisms will give more importance to a certain part of the spectrum and some to others. This is the individuality and the specificity of each human being.

The potential diversity and richness of the human personality is astonishing, and, even on the purely biological level, individual variation is greater in the human than in any other known species. Yet, once again, certain simplifying, universal patterns can be observed. The principal capacities of mind, heart and will give rise, when actualized, to a certain constellation of principal abilities in the human personality. We will now look at these via the following schema (see page 50).

Schema I. The Actualization of the Principal Capacities of the Self

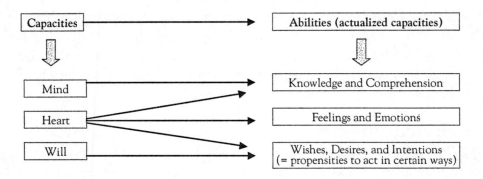

Fig. 2.3. Schema I. The actualization of the principal capacities of the self

Clearly, these various abilities can be further differentiated and classified, but the above categorization will suffice for our present purposes. Thus, a certain complex of understandings, feelings, and intentions is the ultimate, actualized product of the principal capacities of the self. This product emerges gradually as a result of our total life experience, involving innumerable interactions. However, it is reasonable to suppose that some degree of actualization, however minimal, takes place with each interaction. The actualization of a capacity in a given interaction will be called an *instantiation* of that capacity. (An instantiation is thus an ability localized in time.)

In other words, an instantiation is an ability (actualized capacity) that the self displays in a specific interaction. For example, the mind's ability to know may be expressed in a given interaction by the act of perceiving (observing) a given configuration (e.g., the eye sees a dog, the ear hears a barking sound). Similarly, the mind's conceptual ability may be actualized by a specific thought (e.g., this dog seems angry).

At the same time, the discrete actualization of the affective and willing capacities of the self will give rise to certain feelings and desires, which we will lump together under the term *affections*. This, the self may feel the emotion of fear and the desire to run away from the source of fear (i.e., the dog in the above example).

The instantiation of a capacity will generally take place on both a conscious and an unconscious level. However, given the dynamic and spontaneous nature of most interactions, one can assume that instantiations will often be more unconscious than conscious. Thus, after a number of interactions, the self acquires the need for a "summing up" of the results of the interactions. This summation process is itself an interaction (of the self with itself) but, it is perhaps more deliberate, more self-conscious and less spontaneous than the interactions that will have preceded it. We call it the *articulation* of the capacities instantiated by the preceding interactions. This defined, articulations are certain particular (kinds of) instantiations.

We represent the relationship between instantiation and articulation by the following schema.

Schema II. Instantiation/Articulation of the Principal Capacities of the Self

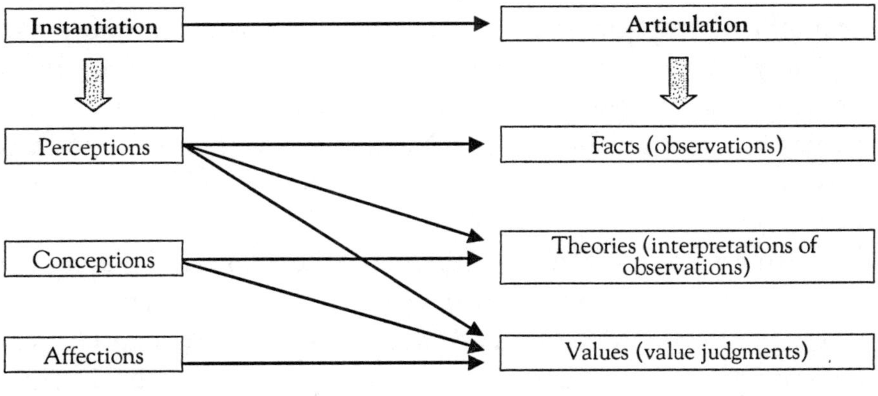

Fig. 2.4. Schema II. Instantiation/articulation of the principal capacities of the self

Perceptions represent the instantiation of our capacity for experience. As indicated in schema I, this capacity is partly mental and partly emotional. Thus, in our framework, observations articulate not only the perception of concrete, sensible objects (e.g., "this apple is red") but also of internal emotional states (e.g., "I am aware that I am now feeling sad"). Observations thus articulate the most primary and direct form of information about our environment (including the inner environment of the self). A single observation corresponds to the popular notion of a "fact," and we will use these terms interchangeably.

Conceptions are instantiations of our capacity for abstract thought and our ability to conceive of configurations and structures we have never actually perceived or observed. Thus, the articulation of concepts may involve observables, but will usually also involve one or more *abstract* terms, i.e., terms referring to non-observable structures, forces, or entities. The statement that "the mind is a capacity of the soul" is a theoretical statement, for neither the mind nor the soul can be directly observed, nor can the binary relation "is a capacity of " be directly perceived.

The importance of concepts is that they allow us to correlate a certain number of diverse perceptions and to conceive of them as deriving from our experience of different aspects of a coherent and unified whole. Theories, then, are explanations for or interpretations of observations. Although theories are of course usually inferred or generalized from observations, it is now known by a theorem of mathematical logic that there are, in general, an infinity of logically incompatible theories consistent with any given finite set of facts. Thus, the gap between perception and conception, fact and theory, is discrete and irreducible. No matter how extensive and careful our observations, there is always a subjective and creative input into any theory.

An affection is the instantiation of the emotional tone of our interaction and the complex of desires and intentions that attend it. On the most primitive level, an affection amounts to a primary experience of pleasure or pain. Its articulation as a value would be "that was pleasant and should be repeated" or "that was unpleasant and should be avoided." However, by the time an individual has actualized enough capacities to articulate instantiations, he will have already developed a *value paradigm*, that is, a theoretical framework in which he interprets his affections. For example, he may be able to say of an experience of drug euphoria, "that felt good but is dangerous and should be avoided in the future at all costs." Thus, when we speak of values, we are referring to those value judgments that result from a complex of experience (perceptions), knowledge (conceptions), and emotions or desires (affections).

Indeed, as our schema II makes clear, the hierarchy of facts, theories, and values is a cumulative hierachy. Facts are at the basis of the hierachy. They are the most simple, direct, and objective. Though observations do involve abstraction and emotional reaction, they are primarily based on direct experience. Moreover, facts relating to concrete (mind-independent) objects are in principle verifiable by all normally endowed human subjects and are thus relatively objective.

Next in complexity are theories, which involve both perceptions and conceptions to a considerable extent. Since there is an irreducible subjective element involved in the formation of concepts, theories are more subjective than facts, and the verification of theories is a rather complex affair. In particular, facts can in principle be independently verified by each observer, but the verification of a theory almost always involves cooperation and intersubjective exchanges among a group of theoreticians.

Finally, values are the most complex of all, involving all the basic capacities of the self. They are also the most subjective, because two individuals may share similar observations and a similar theoretical framework and still, for purely subjective reasons, make opposite value judgments in a given instantiation. Value judgments therefore express the deeper aspects of the self, or soul, as well as involving all of the soul's capacities.

We now define *morality* as the science of value judgments and *moral education* as the process of learning how to make true and effective value judgments. In the following section, we examine briefly what this may mean.

7. Objectivity, Causality, and the Reality Principle

The schemata we have presented in section 6 (see pp. 50 and 51 above) are highly Platonistic, recalling in particular Plato's powerful model of the divided line.[11] Indeed, we can say that instantiations

---

11. Plato (428–348 B.C.) was arguably the greatest of the Athenian philosophers. A disciple of Socrates (470–399 B.C.), Plato popularized and developed Socrates' "theory of

are to articulations as capacities are to abilities, and that instantiations are reflections ("shadows") of capacities while articulations are reflections of abilities. Thus, instantiations particularize capacities and articulations particularize abilities. [12]

But, so far, there is a fundamental difference between our approach and that of Plato. All that we have described pertains fundamentally to the individual self or soul. We have spoken of interactions between the self and the environment and given great attention to the structure of the self, but said very little about the structure of the environment in which this self functions.

One could imagine, for example, that the autonomy and well-being of the individual—thus, his proper development—are a purely personal and subjective affair. In the absence of any confrontation with an objective reality external to the self, one might well conceive that a hallucination of the mind could represent spiritual de-

---

forms" according to which all observable (material) realities are imperfect (or lesser) reflections or "shadows" (copies) of absolute, universal, and unchanging forms. Plato held that the only true knowledge was knowledge of these forms, and in his writings, particularly in *The Republic*, he undertook to instruct his readers in the method of obtaining knowledge of the forms, starting with the dark cave of material reality and gradually ascending into the bright sunlight of spiritual reality. The present work, and chapter 2 in particular, make extensive and deliberate use of Platonic notions.

12. These relationships could be represented diagrammatically as follows:

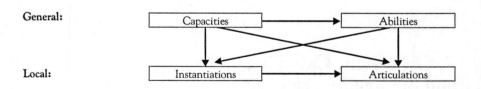

General: Capacities ⟶ Abilities

Local: Instantiations ⟶ Articulations

All arrows, whether horizontal, vertical, or diagonal, represent a relationship of universal to particular. Thus, such relationships exist on the general level (i.e., between capacities and abilities), on the local level (i.e., between instantiations and articulations), and between the general and local levels (e.g., capacities to instantiations and abilities to articulations).

velopment, if the person harboring the illusion felt happy and content. Indeed, such a dismissive view of spirituality is held by many materialists, who regard religion as nothing but a collective neurotic defense mechanism—a child-like clinging to comforting illusions in the face of the reality of a harsh and unpleasant world.

The Bahá'í Writings make it absolutely clear that all of the capacities of the self have been given us by God that we might attain to a true and accurate knowledge of the structure God has Himself inscribed in the innermost recesses of reality (including the reality of our own selves). Thus, the knowledge we seek is not just arbitrary ideas, but knowledge of the *truth* about reality—the way reality is in fact structured. Similarly, our affections must be directed not towards unworthy objects but towards that which is in reality beautiful and worthwhile. And our desires, intentions and actions must be directed towards the truly *good* rather than being self-indulgent performances of our abilities.

Put simply, the capacities of mind, will, and heart, when *properly developed*, give us the ability to discern or recognize truth (the true), to accomplish and pursue goodness (the good) and to love and be faithful to beauty (the beautiful). According to the Bahá'í Writings, the affirmation that God exists as a perfect, absolute, uncaused, all-powerful, omniscient, and all-loving Being means that truth (the structure of reality) has objective existence, that the worth or value of each existing entity relative to any other entity is defined and has objective existence, and that the beauty of a given entity or system exists intrinsically and objectively. We now make this assumption explicit and call it the *objectivity hypothesis*, because it amounts to the assumption that the objects of moral or spiritual knowledge have objective existence and can therefore be authentically pursued. In other words, spiritual and moral knowledge is real, scientific knowledge of certain objective laws of cause and effect which are not just self-induced, purely subjective states of mind.

It should be noted that the current practice of successful science is based on the objectivity hypothesis as applied to facts and theories. We have simply extended this hypothesis to the realm of values, affirming thereby the objective existence of moral reality, and thus of moral truth, and of objective norms as a basis for value choices. On the practical level, this means that value choices have real, observable consequences, some leading to relatively good results (the long-term optimization of happiness and autonomy) and others to relatively bad results (unhappiness and unnaturally restrictive dependencies).

In the final analysis, truth, goodness, and beauty are just different expressions of the nature and attributes of God Himself. Our minds apprehend God as truth, our hearts perceive Him as beauty and love, and our wills as the right and the good. The point is that we discover the reality of truth, goodness and beauty; we do not invent these realities. And, in making this discovery we are fulfilling the basic purpose of our existence, which is the knowledge and love of God.

Interactions are thus encounters with reality and, more particularly, with the *law of cause and effect* that God has inscribed in reality. This law implies that whenever certain conditions A (the cause) are obtained, then certain (usually other) conditions B (the effect) will inevitably follow. When we understand how this law works, we can initiate those actions (causes) that will produce the effect of increasing our happiness and well-being. Spiritual autonomy is precisely the ability to initiate such positive and successful interactions. Thus, it is only because interactions allow us to confront the law of cause and effect in reality that we can achieve the twin goals of moral education—the attainment of well-being and of autonomy. We call this basic feature of the process of moral education *the (spiritual) reality principle*.

In thinking of life as an educational process, we must bear in mind that we are limited, imperfect, and needful creatures, and so our spontaneous reactions to any given encounter with reality are subject to various distortions. These distortions must be eliminated if we are to apprehend the truth, accomplish truly good actions, and have affection for the truly beautiful. Thus, the proper development of the capacities of the self means learning how to separate truth from falsehood, good from evil, and beauty from ugliness. We must learn how to respond to the God-given reality of the world, not our distorted conceptions of it.

8. Inner Models of Reality

As we develop from our initial condition, in which our spiritual capacities are a pure potential, our subjectivity gradually constructs an inner model or image that represents the world as seen through our particular eyes. It is this model of reality, rather than the reality itself, which largely determines how we behave in any given situation.

Since no two individuals have identical life experiences or identical spiritual capacities, no two inner models will be identical. Moreover, because our capacities are limited, each inner model will be incomplete or partial. But, just as importantly, each inner model will inevitably contain various distortions and even blatantly false elements. We need to see why this is so.

Our inner model is based on our articulation—as facts, theories, and values—of input we have received from our interactions with reality. However, we face reality neither as self-sufficient gods nor as infinitely flexible and adaptable beings, but as needful creatues. We therefore cannot receive the input from reality as if we were uninvolved spectators of life. To some degree, we will tend to see reality as we would like it to be rather than as it is. We may, for example, *project our needs* onto reality by incorporating various wished-for elements into our inner model even if they are not present in the data we actually receive from our encounter with reality. Or, we may refuse to acknowledge the evidence of dangerous or threatening elements in our perceptions of reality. In either case, we will speak of a *self-generated* or *need-generated* distortion of our view of reality.

Self-generated distortions can be involved not only in our observations but also in our theories and values. For example, a perfectly innocent remark by a loved one whose approval we seek or an authority figure whose power we fear may give rise to a fantastically distorted interpretation (or theory) concerning what may have motivated the remark.

A second source of distortion in our inner model of reality is *other-generated* rather than self-generated. These distortions arise because much of our information, interpretations, and value judgments about reality come from other subjects who are also needful creatures like ourselves. Thus, what they tell us represents an articulation of their view of reality (their inner model), not reality itself: we may internalize as "facts" certain data that are in reality a highly subjective input from other people.

For example, suppose that, for whatever reason, a mother finds her young daughter's spontaneous singing extremely irritating, and continually berates the child by telling her that "you shouldn't sing because you have a terrible voice." Quite naturally, the child may grow up having internalized as a "fact" that she has a terrible singing voice. If, later on, others find she has a pleasing voice and tell her so, she will have to go through the process of adjusting her distorted inner model to conform to this more accurate feedback from reality.

We can thus see that constructing an accurate inner model of reality is not an easy matter. We must strive to transcend our purely individual perspective, complete our partial picture, eliminate self-generated distortion, and detect and resist other-generated distortions. This can only be accomplished by a ruthless *will to the truth*. We must be utterly dedicated to discovering the truth about all aspects of reality (including the inner reality of the self) and this truth must become the basis of all our interactions with reality. In this connection, 'Abdu'l-Bahá has said:

> Truthfulness is the foundation of all human virtues. Without truthfulness progress and success, in all the worlds of God, are impossible for any soul. When this holy attribute is established in man, all the divine qualities will also be acquired.[13]

Indeed, the will to truth is a fundamental feature of scientific method and the successful practice of science in all contexts. Thus,

---

13. 'Abdu'l-Bahá, quoted in *Advent of Divine Justice*, p. 26.

in a certain sense our approach represents the application of scientific method to the domain of the moral and the spiritual.

Although all our interactions contribute to our picture of reality, certain categories of interactions are more important than others. In particular, the reflexive relationship we each have with our own selves is the central underpinning or key to our overall model of reality. Since all our perceptions of reality are mediated by our subjectivity, the image or model we make of our own selves affects all our perceptions, conceptions, and judgments. For example, if (as is often the case) we have an image of ourselves as inferior to others, then we will systematically exaggerate and multiply perceived threats to the self and dismiss or diminish opportunities for self-enhancement.

Thus, our self-image is the key to our inner model of reality, and our notion of self-worth is the key to our self-image This brings us again back to the notion of intrinsic value discussed in detail in chapter 1.

We will appreciate even more fully the importance of these notions as we discuss and explore, in the next chapter, the implementation of the process of moral development. In particular, we will see that the pursuit of authentic morality proceeds by understanding and then applying the fundamental moral principles underlying each of the categories of interactions of the self with reality.

Chapter 3

Implementing the Development Process

1. Three Paradises

Life is a journey, and everyone begins from the same initial position: total unawareness; absolute unconsciousness. Only after several years of life experience do we slowly emerge from unawareness to awareness. Consciousness is a primal experience of our own being, an irreducible intuition of existence itself. It is our first, primitive step towards autonomy.

The state of unawareness is a paradise of innocence, in which all our needs are satisfied without any effort on our part. We are unaware of our existence and we are unaware of the law of cause and effect by which autonomous individuals are able to act to satisfy their own needs and those of others. However, with the development of autonomy comes an increasing understanding of the *law of causality*: that certain actions on our part will lead to positive and productive consequences and that other actions, under the same conditions, will lead to negative and destructive consequences.

This understanding of the law of cause and effect is the "knowledge of good and evil" spoken of in the Book of Genesis of the Bible.[1]

---

1. See in particular Genesis 2–3.

Indeed, the Bible posits a mythical paradise of Eden as the beginning point for the human race as a whole. This paradise is similar to the paradise of the mother's womb: in Eden all the needs of Adam and Eve were satisfied without any effort on their part. Their expulsion from Eden is clearly a symbolic account of their awakening to self-awareness (e.g., that they were naked) and their confrontation with the law of causality. Moreover, just as Adam and Eve must face a world of pain outside their paradise, so each of us, when once expelled from the blissful conditions of our mother's womb, face a world filled with suffering, both potential and real.

As we acquire greater autonomy in childhood and adolescence, we also increase our awareness of just how much pain and suffering this world can inflict on even the most fortunate of human beings. In the face of this realization, we may naturally have moments when we long to return to the Edenic paradise of ease and innocence. But of course, to return to that paradise would be to lose our growing autonomy and independence, our mature sexual, intellectual, and physical powers.

We therefore conceive of a second, adolescent paradise, one where we have total freedom to act as we please—to seek gratification of all our desires and to indulge all our passions—but without there being any negative consequences. It is thus a paradise of complete freedom and total irresponsibility.

Of course this paradise does not exist and cannot exist. The very law of causality that allows us to gratify our desires or fulfill our needs also dictates that we will suffer whenever we seek such gratification or need fulfillment in an illegitimate manner. The more irresponsibly we use our freedom, the more suffering we bring on ourselves and others.

Misuse of freedom also incurs a decrease in autonomy. This loss of autonomy is experienced in the form of various unnatural dependencies or addictions, which make us prey to impulses that we find difficult or even impossible to resist. In the end, we feel that we "cannot live" without continual sexual gratification, or drugs or alcohol, or the constant approval of others. Abuse of freedom leads to loss of freedom. Moreover, the satisfaction experienced by these temporary gratifications actually diminishes, even as we pursue them more desperately.

The only escape from this vicious cycle of the increasingly desperate pursuit of a steadily diminishing gratification is to replace it by a virtuous cycle of increasing self-mastery. The first stage of this virtuous cycle is to increase our autonomy (self-development) by gaining true and accurate knowledge of the moral law of cause and effect. We must truly understand what are the short and long term consequences of acting, thinking, and feeling in a certain manner. Once this knowledge is achieved, we then feel attracted to the goal of acting rightly, because we now know that this is what will produce our true happiness. This attraction to righteousness is the "love of the truth" so often spoken of in the Holy Scriptures of all religions. (See appendix III for further development of these ideas.)

This love of the truth, this thirst after righteousness, gives us the energy to maintain a sustained motivation or intention to act in accordance with our (increasing) knowledge of the law of causality. Though we may not always be successful in acting in accordance with our knowledge, the very striving to do so gradually produces an inner development—an inner freedom. This inner freedom is the hallmark of the autonomy that is the goal of moral development.

Moreover, as a result of this pure striving, we gradually overcome our previously "uncontrollable" impulses and we gain the power to act in conformity with the law of causality and thereby satisfy our needs in a legitimate manner. This legitimate satisfaction of our needs, both spiritual and material, results in genuine and enduring happiness. As Bahá'u'lláh has said:

> Man's supreme distinction, his real advancement, his final victory, have always depended, and will continue to depend, upon [the ordinances of God]. Whoso keepeth the commandments of God shall attain everlasting felicity.[2]

---

2. Bahá'u'lláh, *Gleanings from the Writings of Bahá'u'lláh*, p. 289.

O ye peoples of the world! Know assuredly that My command-
ments are the lamps of My loving providence among my ser-
vants, and the keys of My mercy for My creatures.[3]

There is thus a third paradise: the paradise of autonomy and responsibility. This paradise is attainable and it brings a true and enduring
happiness. By gaining accurate knowledge of the law of causality
and then by developing the inner freedom to act on the basis of this
knowledge and in conformity with this law, we are able to satisfy all
of our true and healthy needs in a legitimate (i.e., God-ordained)
manner. Moreover, to enter the paradise of autonomous responsibility, we do not have to renounce any of our mature capacities. We
only have to learn to use these capacities in a proper manner.

  Thus, in a certain sense, the process of moral development is
the journey from the irrational and untenable paradise of irrespon-
sible freedom to the lasting and attainable paradise of responsible
autonomy. This journey is possible because God has Himself ordained
the laws that govern this process and has given us all the tools necessary for its successful pursuit. We now turn to an examination of
the basic principles underlying this process.

2. Altruistic Love—the Relationship Between Individuals

You and I, like any two human beings, have a deep, God-created
need to relate authentically to each other. An authentic relationship goes from the center of my being to the center of your being, as
soon as we have each recognized the intrinsic value—the image of
God—in the other. God's image within us is our respective souls and
their inherent capacities of knowing, of loving and of willing. Mutual recognition of intrinsic value enables us to relate in a way that

---

3. Ibid., p. 332.

we each give priority to the legitimate needs of the other rather than to our own needs (whether legitimate or otherwise).

Thus, the trademark of relational authenticity is sincere, unselfish love—a spark that comes from God through each to the other. Such altruistic love makes the other the *end* or *goal* of the relationship. It honors the other as a human being and thus as a representative of the highest value in creation.

We can, of course, relate in many other ways, but they are all just variations of a single theme: we each give priority, however subtly, to our own (perceived) needs over the needs of the other. Whenever present in a relationship, this kind of entrenched egotism negates authenticity, giving rise to manipulation, exploitation, competition, and the mutual search for dominance. In a non-authentic relationship we each seek power—to compel the other to satisfy our needs. Thus, authentic relationships are based on love and non-authentic relationships on power.

The process of relating authentically is an *authentic dialogue* in which we exchange ideas (seek truth together), share emotions, and work collaboratively. Thus, whatever we bring to such a dialogue is used towards the end of establishing an increasingly authentic relationship. When we relate non-authentically, we bring only our needs and it is the other who now becomes a means to their satisfaction. Hence, the pursuit of a non-authentic relationship leads not only to the passive negation of authenticity, but to its active reversal: what was the end has now become the means to a lesser end.

We express our love for others by seeking to satisfy their legitimate needs because this helps develop their soul's God-given potential (as well as our own). But this supposes that we have at least some ability to distinguish between legitimate (or proper) needs and unreasonably selfish desires. The knowledge and implementation of what is appropriate for the development of human potential is *justice*. Justice and love go together: love provides the motivation to serve the other, and justice provides the knowledge necessary for the proper and efficient implementation of this motivation.

Thus, authentic relationships involve not only sincere love for the spiritual reality of others, but also valid knowledge of that reality. When love and justice express themselves in action, then we have all that is necessary for successful dialogue, i.e., for *unity*.

Later on, when we discuss the moral principles underlying relationships within a social group, we will give a much fuller discussion of the equation, unity = love + justice. In the context of the relationship between two individuals, authentic unity is experienced as total reciprocity (justice) and as complete harmony and happiness (love).

We are now ready to formulate explicitly the fundamental moral principle governing the interaction between the self and another individual human. We call this the fundamental principle of one-to-one relationships:

> *In relation to another human being, we should always strive to act in such a manner as to increase the actuality and potentiality of altruistic love.*

This principle means that we must consciously evaluate our actions and attitudes towards others according to whether these actions and attitudes are favorable or unfavorable to an increase in altruistic love. Such evaluation of actions and attitudes is ongoing. It precedes a given action and is then applied again in a retroactive consideration of the actual consequences of the action.

Both pre- and post-evaluation of our actions are necessary. The pre-evaluation tends to assure that our motives and intentions are pure. However, we must realize that the human condition is such that we may fail in a given instance even if our intention was sincere. In such a case, it is not enough to say that we have sincerely tried and that is all one can expect of us. If we truly desire unity and harmony in our relationships, then we must correct our actions and attitudes until such harmony is actually achieved. We are not looking for (even legitimate) excuses for our failures. Rather, we are striving for genuine success.

But what if our post-evaluation leads us to believe that failure truly is the fault of the other? To answer this question we must look somewhat deeper into the essential nature of human relationships.

3. Love, Power, and Justice

That love is the fundamental principle regulating relationships between individuals is clearly and repeatedly stated in the Bahá'í Writings:

> The essence of Bahá'u'lláh's Teaching is all-embracing love, for love includeth every excellence of humankind. It causeth every soul to go forward. It bestoweth on each one, for a heritage, immortal life.[4]

> In every dispensation, there hath been the commandment of fellowship and love, but it was a commandment limited to the community of those in mutual agreement, not to the dissident foe. In this wondrous age, however, praised be God, the commandments of God are not delimited, not restricted to any one group of people, rather have all the friends been commanded to show forth fellowship and love, consideration and generosity and loving-kindness to every community on earth. . . . The meaning of this is that ye must show forth tenderness and love to every human being, even to your enemies, and welcome them all with unalloyed friendship, good cheer, and loving-kindness. When ye meet with cruelty and persecution at another's hands, keep faith with him; when malevolence is directed your way, respond with a friendly heart. To the spears and arrows rained upon you, expose your breasts for a target mirror-bright; and in return for curses, taunts and wounding words, show forth abounding love.[5]

> Wherefore must the loved ones of God associate in affectionate fellowship with stranger and friend alike, showing forth to all the utmost loving-kindness, disregarding the degree of their capacity, never asking whether they deserve to be loved. In every instance let the friends be considerate and infinitely

---

4. 'Abdu'l-Bahá, *Selections from the Writings of 'Abdu'l-Bahá*, no. 31:15.
5. Ibid., no. 7:4.

kind. Let them never be defeated by the malice of the people, by their aggression and their hate, no matter how intense.[6]

> Know ye, verily, that the happiness of mankind lieth in the unity and harmony of the human race, and that spiritual and material developments are conditioned upon love and amity among all men.[7]

Moreover, in such passages as the following, 'Abdu'l-Bahá gives us the fundamental method of achieving such a degree of love in human relationships:

> Love the creatures for the sake of God and not for themselves. You will never become angry or impatient if you love them for the sake of God. Humanity is not perfect. There are imperfections in every human being, and you will always become unhappy if you look toward the people themselves. But if you look toward God, you will love them and be kind to them, for the world of God is the world of perfection and complete mercy. Therefore, do not look at the shortcomings of anybody; see with the sight of forgiveness. The imperfect eye beholds imperfections. The eye that covers faults looks toward the Creator of souls. He created them, . . . they are the signs of His grandeur.[8]

The logic of the last quotation is quite clear. When we look at people "themselves" we see primarily their limitations, which does not evoke our love. But when we see the image of God within (the spiritual reality of) the individual, then we see a true beauty and potential which naturally and effortlessly attracts our love. (Of course, we must deploy conscious efforts in order to see this image of God within the other.)

---

6. Ibid., no. 8:8.
7. Ibid., no. 225:10.
8. 'Abdu'l-Bahá, *Promulgation of Universal Peace*, p. 93.

Moreover, as has been discussed in the previous chapters, this image of God is the objectively-existing soul of the individual. It is not simply our imagination or a mental image. When we perceive the spiritual reality of the other, then we truly love this reality. It is not that we pretend to love the unlovable or that we love the person "in spite of" his unlovable nature. It is rather that we have developed the ability truly to see the beauty in the other and to love the reality of that beauty. As 'Abdu'l-Bahá has put it, we must be ". . . sincerely kind, not in appearance only."⁹

Thus, altruistic love is the fundamental principle of human relations, and this principle is implemented on the basis of true perception and knowledge of the spiritual reality within ourselves and others. This love has both an active and a passive component. The passive component expresses itself in our total acceptance of the other, without prejudgment or preconditions. The active component is our vital and proactive concern for the welfare of the other. Love is acceptance plus concern.

Though it may seem difficult to conceive at first, the two components of love are quite independent of each other. This is due to the extreme flexibility of human nature. Acceptance without concern is what is usually called *tolerance*, while concern without acceptance is *conditional love*. Tolerance occurs when we renounce the desire to change, convert, or dominate the other but have not yet developed the capacity to work actively for the improvement of his or her well-being. Conditional love means that, while we have recognized the spiritual potential of the other and are concerned for the development of that potential, we have not yet reconciled ourselves to what we perceive as the other's limitations.

Since authentic love involves both components, it is unconditional and is the goal towards which we are striving. Nevertheless, we can appreciate the fact that any degree of love is better than its absence. On the one hand, tolerance is better than rejection or ha-

---

9. 'Abdu'l-Bahá, *Selections from the Writings of 'Abdu'l-Bahá*, no. 1:7.

tred, and in many situations of social conflict, the establishment of genuine tolerance is recognized by all as a significant achievement. On the other hand, parental love can sometimes be conditional. The mother and father may be sincerely concerned for improving the welfare of the child, and make many sacrifices to that end, but they may be unable accept the child's limitations (perhaps, because they perceive the child as an extension of themselves and thus the child's limitations as a reflection of their own).

Of course, there remains a fundamental problem. Given the fact that, for the most part, human relations are currently based on selfish interests rather than altruistic love, how are we to move from the present configuration to the intended one? This is the true problem of moral development. We must therefore address the question of why selfishness and powerseeking seem to predominate over love in human relationships.

One answer often given to this question is that we humans are selfish and aggressive because it is our intrinsic nature: we literally *cannot* be otherwise. Indeed, a number of materialist philosophers and scientists have actively propagated the view that we are genetically programmed to be selfish and aggressive, and that the best we can do in the face of this "fact" is to arrange our society so that the inevitable discharge of our ego-aggressive drives and impulses does the least possible social damage. The many historical examples of intraspecific aggression and human cruelty are frequently adduced as conclusive evidence of the thesis that humans are inherently and ineradicably selfish and aggressive. From this point of view, true altruism does not and cannot exist, and attempts to implement altruistic love as the basis of human relationships are doomed to failure.

Refuting this pessimistic view of human nature is easy once one understands clearly what the thesis really asserts. In the first place, no one doubts that humans are capable of the most extreme cruelty and aggression towards each other, as is proved conclusively by a mere glance at history or current events. What the materialistic thesis asserts is that humans are incapable of anything else (though aggressive motives may be sometimes cleverly disguised as sincere concern for others). However, the same history that is so replete with evil is also replete with examples of genuine altruism and self-sacrifice.

One of my personal favorites is the example of the Roman senator who, upon conversion to Christianity, deliberately sold himself into slavery in order to replace, and thus free from slavery, the only son of a (non-Christian) widow. Such clear acts of deliberate self-sacrifice cannot be reasonably interpreted as disguised selfishness or aggression. The three centuries of persecution willingly endured by the first generations of Christians, or the more historically recent persecution endured by the Bahá'ís of Iran, are other examples. Besides these dramatic examples, there are such perennial examples as the daily sacrifices of mothers for their children in all cultures all over the world.

Indeed, some anthropologists, Richard Leakey for example, have pointed out that the capacity for social cooperation and mutuality was the dominant factor—much more important than intelligence—in enabling early humans to survive and prevail against animal competitors who were physically superior to humans in every conceivable respect: strength, acuity of perception, and fleetness of foot. Furthermore, Leakey points out, the operation of natural selection would take only a few generations to destroy any species that was genetically programmed for intraspecific aggression.[10] One can hardly imagine a more negatively selective gene than one that predisposes those who carry it to destroy or be destroyed by all others who carry it. Thus, if there ever was such a species, it has long since disappeared from the earth, and it is certainly not, therefore, the human species.

In its statement, *The Promise of World Peace*, addressed to the peoples of the world, the Universal House of Justice has dealt with the materialistic thesis in the following terms:

Indeed, so much have aggression and conflict come to characterize our social, economic and religious systems, that many have

---

10. See R. Leakey and R. Lewin, *People of the Lake*, New York: Doubleday, 1978.

succumbed to the view that such behavior is intrinsic to human nature and therefore ineradicable. . . .

. . . Dispassionately examined, the evidence reveals that such conduct, far from expressing man's true self, represents a distortion of the human spirit. Satisfaction on this point will enable all people to set in motion constructive social forces which, because they are consistent with human nature, will encourage harmony and co-operation instead of war and conflict.

To choose such a course is not to deny humanity's past but to understand it.[11]

We thus come to another basic principle of our program: *the human being is capable both of extreme cruelty and extreme altruism.* Any satisfactory theory of human nature and behavior will have to account for both these capacities. Since the materialistic thesis does not do this, we reject it as unscientific (it does not explain the facts of human existence). But this returns us to our original question: how can we explain the frequency and extent of conflict and aggression in our history?

The answer derives from the Bahá'í view of history as a collective growth process, destined in time to culminate in the unification of humanity and the organization of the world's peoples into a planetary society based on spiritual principles. Bahá'u'lláh explains that humanity is currently at the stage of adolescence, the stage of transition to the mature adult configuration of world unity.[12]

It follows that our past is the history of our collective childhood. For the individual, childhood is the period when one moves from a position of total weakness, dependency, and vulnerability to a position of relative strength and independence. The individual experiences this process as an accretion of power, and he may easily

---

11. Universal House of Justice, *The Promise of World Peace: To the People's of the World,* pp. 15–16.

12. See for example Shoghi Effendi's extensive discussions of this question, based on appropriate citations from the works of Bahá'u'lláh, in *The World Order of Bahá'u'lláh.*

become preoccupied with the process of *acquiring* greater and greater power rather than the process of learning to use his power in an appropriate manner: gradually and subtly, the pursuit of power becomes the focus of life.

In a similar manner, the collective childhood of humanity has been characterized by the pursuit of power, and this pursuit is the root cause of the prevalence of conflict and injustice in our history. Indeed, we inherit a history of injustice in which the strong have consistently dominated the weak: men have dominated women, more powerful tribes and nations have conquered and enslaved weaker ones, war has predominated over peace, and physical and military power have predominated over intellectual prowess and social harmony.

That the pursuit of power is the root cause of past injustices has been explicitly recognized by Bahá'u'lláh in such terms as the following: "Ever since the seeking of preference and distinction came into play, the world has been laid waste. It hath become desolate."[13]

Notice that what is deemed the cause of injustice is the *seeking* of power, not power itself. Without power we can do nothing, neither good nor evil. The error lies in pursuing power for its own sake—making power the end rather than the means of pursuing moral and socially productive ends: "Indeed, man is noble inasmuch as each one is a repository of the sign of God. Nevertheless, to regard oneself as superior in knowledge, learning or virtue, or to exalt oneself or seek preference, is a grievous transgression."[14] In other words, each of us may well possess a certain degree of power, but to use that power to establish our dominance over others constitutes a moral and spiritual error. To pursue power is to misuse power.

We may of course misuse power without pursuing power. For example, we may harm someone by the exercise of our power even though we sincerely intend to do good (e.g., a surgeon who sincerely tries to heal but makes a professional mistake). Such misuses of power

---

13. Bahá'u'lláh, quoted in *Messages from the Universal House of Justice: 1963–1986*, no. 206:3a.

14. Bahá'u'lláh, quoted in *Messages*, no. 206:3b.

are an inevitable part of the process of learning how to use power appropriately. But the pursuit of power for its own sake is always wrong, because the very intention is itself immoral, regardless of the external consequences.

This raises the question of the appropriate use of power. In particular, we seem to face the following paradoxical situation. We have declared that our goal (our pursuit) is altruistic love, but power cannot command or create love. Indeed, one of the great contradictions of human existence is that we often persist in attributing so great a value to power even when we have already learned through bitter experience that power is itself utterly incapable of producing the most valuable thing of all, i.e., love. What, then, is the moral use of power, and in particular, how can the exercise of power serve the pursuit of altruistic love?

The answer is that power can be used to create and establish justice. Once established, justice provides the conditions under which love can flourish. (Love may be born in the absence of justice, but it cannot endure in the face of continuing injustice.) Thus, the moral use of power is in the pursuit of justice. Let us examine this in more detail.

If you act unjustly towards me, I have basically three possible responses. The first is to seek revenge, to use my power to make you suffer in the same way that you have made me suffer. This is a "power response," and it is one that often appears the most natural to us, given the history of powerseeking we all inherit. Indeed, the power response is so spontaneous that it usually takes considerable self-insight and self-control to avoid it.

The second response is to do nothing, to suffer the injustice in silence. One then becomes a victim, either because one is too weak to do otherwise or because one is too afraid to use what power one has to seek revenge. This is the "victim response" to injustice.

The third response is to seek justice. This response can take a number of forms. On one end of the spectrum is the possibility of confronting the injustice and denouncing it openly. The other extreme is to oppose the injustice with active love, as described above by 'Abdu'l-Bahá. All of the subtle combinations of love and justice between these two extremes leave room for immense personal creativity in dealing with injustice. The third response to injustice is thus the "unity response," because it involves an appropriate combination of love and justice.

Once we have clearly understood what is involved, virtually every personal encounter with another, whether initially positive or negative, provides us opportunity for an original and creative response, a response which will take us a step forward in our process of moral development.

However, we stand in need of some principle that will allow us to determine when the unity response should be more weighted in favor of justice or in favor of love. 'Abdu'l-Bahá has provided us with just such a criterion:

> O ye beloved of the Lord! The Kingdom of God is founded upon equity and justice, and also upon mercy, compassion, and kindness to every living soul. Strive ye then with all your heart to treat compassionately all humankind—except for those who have some selfish, private motive, or some disease of the soul. Kindness cannot be shown the tyrant, the deceiver, or the thief, because, far from awakening them to the error of their ways, it maketh them to continue in their perversity as before. No matter how much kindliness ye may expend upon the liar, he will but lie the more, for he believeth you to be deceived, while ye understand him too well, and only remain silent out of your extreme compassion.[15]

Thus, our response to individual evil is governed not so much by the degree of injustice perpetrated against us, or even by the other's active intention to harm, but rather by the educative effectiveness of the response. We must respond in a manner that maximizes the likelihood of the perpetrator gaining effective insight into the nature of his or her own moral condition.

---

15. 'Abdu'l-Bahá, *Selections from the Writings of 'Abdu'l-Bahá*, no. 138:1.

If we consider the body of statements in the Bahá'í Writings dealing with this question, it appears that in the majority of cases our response should be to oppose active love to provocative injustice. However, in cases which involve a deliberate attempt to deceive or manipulate others, confrontation and denunciation may be morally necessary.

Also, if the unjust act of the other is directed not at us but at an innocent and weaker third party, then the moral equation changes. We can choose for ourselves to return good for evil but we cannot impose our personal choice on others. Our moral duty to protect the innocent may thus require us to respond with justice when we would have chosen mercy had only we ourselves been the object of the unjust act.

Clearly, we may not know in the beginning whether we are dealing with a person who is a deceiver. Thus, a reasonable strategy seems to be to respond initially with kindness and compassion. If further encounters with the individual give us hard evidence or clear indications of an intent to deceive, we can then generate a response more weighted in favor of justice. But if we allow the "justice response" to become the habitual first response to any aggressive behavior on the part of others, then we will miss many occasions for our own spiritual development and we will probably slip easily into the power response under the guise of seeking justice.

This raises the following sharp question: why is the power response unjust? Why am I not justified in seeking revenge for an undeserved hurt that has been done me by another? What is the difference between seeking revenge and seeking justice?

The answer lies in the observation that revenge simply perpetrates another injustice in response to the initial one. Compounding injustice with another injustice is not going to reduce the incidence of injustice in the world, but increase it. The revenge response perpetuates a spiral of action and reaction that can continue for a lifetime, for generations, for centuries, even for millennia (as has indeed happened in history).

The point is that *we cannot change or undo the past*. We can only change the future by acting, in the present, in a manner different from the past. Nothing can be clearer than the fact that if we continue to act today as we have acted until now, our future will simply be a continuation of our past.

The revenge response seeks to undo the past by returning to an "even" situation in which we each have the same moral balance sheet towards the other. But this is simply impossible. If, for example, you have injured my pet dog, how can we say that for me now to perpetrate a similar act towards you will restore the balance? How can the pain you have caused me be measured or compensated by the pain I would then cause you?

Maybe, for example, I am much more attached to my pet than you are to yours. What then? How much damage must I do to be certain of causing the same degree of pain you have caused me? I will have to examine your life, seek out your attachments and weak points, and deliberately perpetrate an act that causes you sufficient pain. But what if I overshoot the mark? In that case I now have a "pain debt" towards you.

Of course, in reality a revenge seeker never attempts to make such fine calculations. One simply maximizes the damage done in retaliation, in order to "show" the other that one is a force to be reckoned with. But, as we have seen, this only evokes a maximum response in further retaliation, and the spiral continues.

The justice response recognizes and accepts the fact that, however grievous the injustice initially perpetrated, the past cannot be undone. Rather, the justice response seeks to change what can really be changed, namely the future. Specifically, *our personal response to an injustice committed against us by an individual seeks to maximize the likelihood that the individual in question (and/or others) will acquire a sincere motivation not to repeat the injustice in the future.* In some instances this is best done by confronting and denouncing the injustice, perhaps seeking social sanctions for the act. In other instances a response of active kindness on our part will more easily awaken the person to his moral condition.

Let us examine this more closely by addressing the following clear question: what can and does produce long-term changes of behavior and attitudes in human adults? There is only one answer to this question: *self-motivation*. Indeed, whereas the behavior of children can be changed through an appropriate combination of reward and punishment, adult behavior changes only when, as a result of certain life experiences, the adult acquires a sincere determination to change. The key to improving adult–adult relationships thus lies in our understanding that only we have ultimate control over our own behavior and that we have very little control over the behavior of other adults. This means that *the surest way to change a one-on-one relationship is to change our behavior in that relationship*.

The above principle is more particularly true when it comes to long-term, intimate relationships. Suppose, for example, that you have a difficult, complicated relationship with your mother. There is clearly mutual love but, over the years, you have established a relational pattern in which you each have ways of "getting" the other. Whenever your mother acts in such a manner, your response is to protest "why do you always have to do this (e.g., treat me like I was still a child, embarrass me in front of my friends, give me unwanted advice)?" And your mother's most likely response will be to say that if you resent her obvious expressions of love and concern, then perhaps you do not really love and appreciate her as you should.

In overcoming such entrenched patterns, we have to realize that long-term relationships have a history in which each person in the relationship seeks a certain "payoff" or outcome from his or her behavior. For example, it may be that the very reason your mother treats you like a child is so that you will protest and then she can make you feel guilty about lacking appropriate love and appreciation towards her.

In such a case, the most effective way to break the unhealthy pattern is for you to generate a *paradoxical response*. If you act completely different from the past and fail to give the anticipated or expected response, then your mother will be forced to act differently. If, to take a simple example, you do not protest but thank her for her (unwanted) advice (not hypocritically, but because you truly appreciate the motivation behind it), then she can hardly criticize you for being unappreciative. She will be confronted with a new situation where, in any case, she *cannot* continue to act as in the past because the corresponding behavior on your part is no longer forthcoming.

Thus, when 'Abdu'l-Bahá counsels us to "show forth abounding love" in return for "curses, taunts and wounding words" (see p. 67), He is not telling us to become naive victims of others' injustice. He is rather giving us the key to an appropriate response that will break entrenched patterns of injustice, establish new patterns of mutual harmony, and lead ultimately to our enduring happiness and well-being.

The bitter experience of continual conflict in our history should, at the very least, make us willing to try 'Abdu'l-Bahá's approach. After all, if we try it and don't like it, we can always return to the daily round of mutual criticism, struggle, and unhappiness to which we are already accustomed.

There is no doubt that, depending on the circumstances involved, it can take considerable moral courage to generate the appropriate unity response in human relations. For example, if our response to a particular act of injustice towards us is weighted in favor of mercy and kindness, others may well perceive us as weak and helpless victims. We may then be goaded into a power response because we feel it will elicit the approval of others, who tell us we have a "right" to seek revenge. Only our emerging moral autonomy will allow us to disregard such social pressures and to act in a deliberate manner according to principles we have freely chosen.

An alternative to the revenge variation of the power response is the "blame response." We claim we are ready to forgive and forget the past *provided* the other is willing to acknowledge the unjustness of his actions and ask our forgiveness. This may at first appear to be a love response, but it clearly contradicts 'Abdu'l-Bahá's principle that we show to others "the utmost loving-kindness, disregarding the degree of their capacity, never asking whether they deserve to be loved." (See p. 67.) After all, it is easy to love the lovable or the sincerely contrite; loving the unlovable is the real moral challenge. Indeed, it is in striving to generate a love response to injustice that we make the most growth towards moral autonomy and authenticity, which constitute the fundamental goal of our moral striving in the first place.

In any case, a love that puts preconditions is not altruistic love, because altruistic love is unconditional in its very nature (as we have seen above). Our conditional love, though better than seeking revenge, is still an attempt to gain power over the other by forcing him to acknowledge our moral superiority. (In some instances it may even turn out that an unconditional love response on our part was a crucial factor in finally leading the other to acknowledge his injustice.)

More generally, the blame response is a power response because it still looks to the past, requiring that some sort of retro-corrective action take place as a precondition for changing the relationship. The true love response looks only to the future. No matter what the history of a relationship may be—no matter how fraught with injustice—the individuals involved are free to choose, *at any moment,* to change the future history of their relationship by acting differently towards one another. The tyranny of the past is only in our minds; otherwise it has no existence.

Let us sum up. We inherit a history of powerseeking behavior, which has created injustice and thereby reduced both the actuality and potentiality of altruistic love in human relationships. We must reverse this pyramid and deliberately seek altruistic love instead of power. We do this by using our power to establish justice. Once established, justice provides the conditions under which altruistic love can flourish and endure. In the past, we have sought power and sacrificed justice and thus love in the process. We must now seek unity (love and justice) and sacrifice (make use of) power in the process.

Thus, *the conscious renunciation of the pursuit of power* is the key to establishing altruistic love in our relationships with others. Every time we are confronted with a situation in which we are tempted to generate a power response (or a victim response), we must strive instead to generate a unity response. The resistance we all feel to abandoning the pursuit of power is a measure of how deeply powerseeking has become entrenched in our individual and collective psyche.

Our discussion of the implementation of the principle of altruistic love in one-to-one relationships has dealt primarily with the problem of generating an appropriate response to aggressive or unjust gestures on the part of others. However, there is much that we can do proactively to express our love for others. In particular, we can encourage or praise them instead of blaming or criticizing them.

Indeed, part of our legacy of powerseeking behavior is our tendency to use blame and criticism to control and limit the power of others. However, such negativism towards others undermines altruistic love, and once we have consciously renounced the pursuit of power, we no longer need such strategies. Not only should we simply renounce blame and criticism, we should replace them by active praise and encouragement. In fact, one major strategy for generating a paradoxical response (see p. 78) is to praise or encourage when blame is expected.

Criticism is often justified as "constructive" and thus an expression of authentic concern for the other. The logic of justice forces us to acknowledge that, in some contexts, criticism can indeed be necessary and constructive (e.g., to warn the other of danger or to protect him from persisting in doing active harm to himself or third parties). However, the instances when criticism, however well meant, is truly constructive are much rarer than most of us claim.

There are certain social contexts in which I may be perceived as having a "right" to criticize or blame you. However, even if I do have such a right, I can choose freely not to exercise it if I feel that the principle of altruistic love will be better served by silence or by praise and encouragement instead.

The point in any case is that we should always pursue active and authentic love by looking for opportunities to encourage others rather than by seeking some justification for criticizing them. If we do that consistently, then the few times when criticism appears necessary, it is more likely to be authentically constructive.

In attempting to implement the principle of altruistic love in our relationships with others, we must of course be realistic in our expectations. Success comes slowly and with great effort at first—then more quickly and with less effort—but is never total. We humans will never become perfect.

It is, however, quite realistic to expect that we can practically achieve a degree of development such that love and justice completely predominate over powerseeking and conflict in all our relationships. It is a grave mistake to think that such a thing is so ideal as to be unachievable by all save a few "saints" or spiritual exceptions.

We should nonetheless always strive for the absolute ideal and measure the results of our efforts against the principle of pure altruism. For if we do not, we will soon find that subtle compromises creep into our evaluations, leading us to accept much less than is practically achievable.

4. The Existence of God

In the foregoing, there has been much talk of the causality relationship and the fundamental role it plays in the whole process of moral and spiritual development. We need now to take a closer look at some of the general logical properties of this relationship, as well as the logical connections between causality and a few other fundamental relations. Our purpose in undertaking this study is to establish the existence of God on a totally objective basis, as a necessary logical feature of the overall structure of reality itself.[16]

---

16. We have already observed (cf. chapter 1 above) that an authentic relationship with God constitutes the very basis of authentic morality. However, there is a widespread conception that knowledge of God's existence can only be based on subjective emotions or an act of "blind faith." By establishing God's existence in an objective and logical manner we seek to implement 'Abdu'l-Bahá's definition of faith as ". . . first, conscious knowledge, and second, the practice of good deeds." (*Bahá'í World Faith*, p. 383) Once we have attained to the conscious knowledge of God's existence, we have fulfilled the first of 'Abdu'l-Bahá's conditions of faith and can then proceed to the second stage, which is "good deeds," i.e., the establishment of an appropriate (authentic), ongoing dialogue (relationship) with God. For more on the proof of the existence of God, see appendix II, pp. 139–141.

By the term *reality* we mean the totality of existence, everything there is (or was or will be). A *phenomenon* is some (nonempty) portion of reality, and causality is a logical relationship between two phenomena A and B, which holds whenever A is a cause of B (symbolized A → B).[17] This means that A contains a *sufficient reason* for the existence of B. More generally, we hold that any phenomenon B must either be preceded by a cause A different from B (A → B and A ≠ B), or else contain within itself a sufficient reason for its existence (B → B). In the former case, we say that B is *caused* or *other-caused* and in the latter *uncaused* or *self-caused*. The principle that every phenomenon must either be caused or uncaused (and not both) is the *principle of sufficient reason*.

Another basic relation between phenomena is the relation of part to whole: we write A ∈ B whenever the *entity* A is a *component* of the *system* (composite phenomenon) B. Notice that A *may* also be composite, but *must* be an entity (not just an arbitrary system) in order to be a component of another system B (whether the latter is an entity or not). Two systems (whether entities or not) may also be related by one being a *subsystem* of the other. We write A ⊂ B whenever A is a subsystem of B. This means precisely that every component E ∈ A is also a component E ∈ B. For example, a single leaf would be a component of a tree, but all the leaves together would constitute a subsystem of the tree. If E is either a component or subsystem of B, then E is a *part* of B.

From the strictly logical point of view, the defining or characteristic feature of an entity A is that A can be a component of some system B, A ∈ B. In other words, entities *are* components while systems *have* components (they are composite phenomena). Moreover, some systems also are components. Thus, with respect to composition, we have three distinct categories of phenomena. A phenomenon may be noncomposite (have no components), in which case it is necessarily an entity. A phenomenon may be a composite entity,

---

17. Professional philosophers should take note here of my somewhat broader (and thus slightly nonstandard) definition of the term "phenomenon." This usage is consistent throughout the present work.

in which case it both has components and is a component. Or, a phenomenon may be composite without being an entity, in which case it has components but can never be a component.

Causality and composition are related to each other by the obvious *potency principle*, which says that if $A \rightarrow B$, then A must also be a cause of E, where E is any component or any subsystem of B. In other words, to be a cause of B is to be a cause of every part of B—its components and its subsystems. This means that our notion of causality is that of *complete cause* (philosophy recognizes several different notions of "cause").

Finally, the existence of a whole system obviously cannot precede the existence of its components (rather, the constitution of a whole obviously supposes and depends upon the prior or simultaneous existence of its components). We thus have the *principle of limitation*, which asserts that, for every composite phenomenon A, A cannot be a cause of any of its components.

It follows immediately from these principles that no composite phenomenon can be self-caused, for suppose $A \rightarrow A$ where A is composite. Then, by the potency principle $A \rightarrow E$, where E is any component of A. But this contradicts the limitation principle.

In fact, from these valid principles of causality and composition, we can logically deduce the existence of a unique, noncomposite, self-caused, universal cause G. This entity, whose existence we prove, is God (by logical definition). This God is not some abstract figment of our imagination but the actual, ultimate cause of all phenomena and entities, the origin of all being.

Since the proof is easy, we give it here in full. However, the reader who already accepts and understands the existence of a universal uncaused cause (i.e., God) can safely skip the details of the proof without diminishing his or her understanding of the subsequent sections of the course.

Let V be the collection (universe) of *all* entities. Since V is composite it cannot be self-caused (see above) and so must have a cause G (different from V itself). Thus, $G \rightarrow V$, $G \neq V$. Moreover, every phenomenon A is either an entity, and thus a component of V, or else a system all of whose components are in V—in which case

A is a subsystem of V. Thus, G is either a component or a subsystem of V. But, in either case, G → G by the potency principle. Thus, G is self-caused and hence noncomposite (no composite can be self-caused as shown above). Finally, since G → V and every phenomenon A is a part of V, then by the potency principle, G is a universal cause (the cause of every phenomenon, including itself).

Finally, we show that G is the only uncaused phenomenon, for suppose there is another such phenomenon G'. Then G → G' (since G is a universal cause). But since G' is self-caused it cannot be other-caused by the principle of sufficient reason. Thus, G = G' and the uniqueness of G is established.

This clear, logical proof of God's existence and uniqueness is due in its essentials to the great Muslim philosopher Avicenna (ibn Sina, 980–1037). By making use of a few notions of modern logic, our presentation here somewhat simplifies Avicenna's exposition.[18]

The relationships of causality and composition, and the logical connections between them, give us the knowledge of God's existence. This naturally raises the further question of God's nature (what is God like?). To answer this, we need now to consider the value relation $\geq$, mentioned in chapter 1, and which only holds between (i.e., is meaningful for) entities. To say that the entity A is as valuable as the entity B, $A \geq B$, means that A is either more *refined* (higher)—or at least no less refined—than B.

For example, in the physical world, humans are higher (more complex) than animals, animals higher than plants, and plants higher than minerals (inorganic substances). In the spiritual world, the relationship of higher to lower is the relationship of universal to particular (e.g., the relationship between the form of the human in the mind of God, embodied in the Manifestations, and any particular individual human soul).

The fundamental logical connection between causality and value is given by the *refinement principle*: where A and B are entities,

---

18. For an extended discussion of this proof and its historical context, see *The Law of Love Enshrined*, pp. 19–42.

if A → B then A ≥ B. This means that any causal entity must be at least as refined as its effect. Since God is the unique universal cause, God is also the most refined entity in existence.

In particular, humans have the positive qualities of consciousness, intelligence, feelings, and will. Moreover, although each human soul has these qualities to a specific, finite, and limited degree, there is no limit to the degree that these qualities can exist generally in human beings. (For example, no matter how intelligent a given human being may be, it is possible for another human to be more intelligent.) Since God is the unique cause of every human being, God must have these positive qualities (and undoubtedly others) to a degree greater than every limited (finite) degree, thus to an unlimited (infinite) degree. Hence, God is infinitely conscious, infinitely knowing, infinitely loving, and infinitely willing (all-powerful). In fact, since God is the only Being whose existence is absolute (i.e., uncaused), God has these qualities to an absolute degree.

Thus, the logical answer to the question "what is God's nature?" is to say that "God is like us except for possessing none of our limitations and all of our positive qualities to an infinite degree." Of course we cannot really imagine what it means to possess such qualities as consciousness or will to an infinite degree, but the refinement principle does nevertheless gives us at least a minimal, purely logical notion of God's nature.

5. Our Relationship with God

To have a relationship with God we must, of course, know God. Indeed, in chapter 1 we have already seen that knowledge and love of God are the very purpose of our existence. However, it frequently happens that talk about God leads quickly to talk about believing in God. In this way, the focus changes from the objective question of the existence and nature of God to subjective, psychological questions about human beliefs.

That belief in God is not the issue can be clearly seen from the following observation: if God did not exist, then all the belief of all the believers in history would not bring Him into existence; and since He does exist, all the disbelief and doubt of all the atheists and agnostics of history does not diminish in the least His existence. We must therefore strive to *know* that God exists and who God is, not just to have proper beliefs about God. As 'Abdu'l-Bahá has said:

> Day and night you must strive that you may attain the significances of the heavenly Kingdom, perceive the signs of Divinity, acquire certainty of knowledge and realize that this world has a Creator, a Vivifier, a Provider, an Architect—knowing this through proofs and evidences and not through susceptibilities, nay, rather through decisive arguments and real vision—that is to say, visualizing it as clearly as the outer eye beholds the sun. In this way may you behold the presence of God and attain to the knowledge of the holy, divine Manifestations.[19]

Elsewhere, 'Abdu'l-Bahá makes it clear that rational proofs of the existence of God, though necessary, are only part of an overall, integrated process of spiritual and intellectual development:

> If thou wishest the divine knowledge and recognition, purify thy heart from all beside God, be wholly attracted to the ideal, beloved One; search for and choose Him and apply thyself to rational and authoritative arguments. For arguments are a guide to the path and by this the heart will be turned unto the Sun of Truth. And when the heart is turned unto the Sun, then the eye will be opened and will recognize the Sun through the Sun itself. Then man will be in no need of arguments (or proofs), for the Sun is altogether independent, and absolute independence is in need of nothing, and proofs are one of the things of which absolute independence has no need.[20]

---

19. 'Abdu'l-Bahá, *Promulgation*, p. 227.
20. 'Abdu'l-Bahá, in *Bahá'í World Faith*, pp. 383–384. The passage quoted here is from a tablet of 'Abdu'l-Bahá which has not yet been authenticated.

But what practical knowledge of God can we actually derive from our proof? The proof tells us that God is the ultimate cause and ground of all being, including our own. In other words, *everything that exists depends absolutely on God, whether directly or indirectly.* In particular, human beings depend absolutely on God. However, in all creation, only human beings are endowed with consciousness. Thus, we are the only creatures of God who have the capacity *to be aware of our dependency on God.* This, then, gives us the fundamental moral principle governing our relationship with God:

> *In relationship to God, whatever increases our awareness of our dependency on Him is good, and whatever hides or veils from us the knowledge of the ways we are dependent on Him is bad.*

'Abdu'l-Bahá confirms this principle in such terms as the following:

> Existence is of two kinds: one is the existence of God which is beyond the comprehension of man. He, the invisible, the lofty and the incomprehensible, is preceded by no cause but rather is the Originator of the cause of causes. He, the Ancient, hath had no beginning and is the all-independent. The second kind of existence is the human existence. It is a common existence, comprehensible to the human mind, is not ancient, is dependent and hath a cause to it. The mortal substance does not become eternal and vice-versa; the human kind does not become a Creator and vice versa. The transformation of the innate substance is impossible.[21]

What we have called "awareness of our dependency on God" is what is usually called "faith in God." The difference is that, traditionally, faith is conceived as a form of belief, whereas we have defined it as a form of knowledge, i.e., knowledge of how we are dependent on God. Thus, growth in faith is usually considered as acquiring stronger be-

---

21. 'Abdu'l-Bahá, *Selections from the Writings of 'Abdu'l-Bahá*, no. 30:1.

lief, whereas we conceive it as an increase in knowledge: the basis of true faith is true knowledge not blind belief. As 'Abdu'l-Bahá has said: "By faith is meant, first, conscious knowledge, and second, the practice of good deeds."[22]

The next question, of course, is how we go about implementing our principle. How do we act so as to increase our faith, our awareness of our dependency on God? The essential answer to this question is: prayer. We must learn to commune daily with God and thus become aware of His continual presence in our lives. Indeed, our physical bodies come from God only indirectly, through the process of reproduction He has created in the material world, but our souls come directly from God. It is through prayer that we can establish a conscious relationship between our souls and God.

The following short prayer from the Bahá'í Writings is an excellent example of the kind of communion with God that increases awareness of our dependency upon Him. Its wholly non-denominational character makes it appropriate for anyone of whatever faith or belief, and it can be said frequently during the day in almost any circumstance.

> I bear witness, O My God, that Thou hast created me to know Thee and to worship Thee. I testify, at this moment, to my powerlessness and to Thy might, to my poverty and to Thy wealth.
> There is none other God but Thee, the Help in Peril, the Self-Subsisting.[23]

Because dependency on God is an objective feature of reality, increasing our awareness of that dependency is part of our general will to the truth. However, there are in fact extremely practical reasons for giving attention to our relationship with Him, because an authentic relationship with God is the ultimate basis of all other authentic relationships.

---

22. 'Abdu'l-Bahá, in *Bahá'í World Faith*, p. 383.
23. Bahá'u'lláh, in *Bahá'í Prayers: A Selection of Prayers Revealed by Bahá'u'lláh, The Báb, and 'Abdu'l-Bahá*, p. 4.

Indeed, as was evident from the discussion of the principle of altruistic love in sections 2 and 3 above, generating an authentic love response in human relationships requires considerable spiritual energy. The only possible source of this energy in human affairs is a higher power that possesses unlimited spiritual resources. This power is, of course, God.

More particularly, we can understand that awareness of our dependency on God is also awareness of our own weakness and need. Thus, we increase our receptivity to spiritual input from God as we increase our faith in God. Similarly, the more we strive to implement the principle of altruistic love in our relationships with other people, the more keenly we will feel our inadequacies, and the more wholeheartedly we will turn to God in conscious dependency. There is thus a mutual reinforcement of authenticity between our lateral relationships with other people, on one hand, and our vertical relationship with God, on the other.

More generally, as we examine the principles underlying each category of interaction, we will see that every type of authentic relationship depends directly or indirectly on our relationship with God. Also, as we pursue authentic relationships, we stand in need of concrete examples of highly perfected human beings who can show us by their lives how various moral virtues can be actualized. Thus, the prophets and saints of history provide God-given examples of self-sacrificing love and courage in action. To study the life history of, say, Jesus, Buddha, Bahá'u'lláh, or 'Abdu'l-Bahá is to get a direct insight into what such notions as infinite love, infinite compassion, or infinite humility might mean. Such examples, and the insights we derive from them, open up our moral imagination and give us courage to persevere in the path of authentic morality.

6. Our Relationship to Society and to Social Groups

In section 2 of this chapter we have seen that the principle governing a one-to-one relationship (a relationship between two individuals) is altruistic love. We want now to examine the more complex relationship between the individual self and a social group. We call this a "one-many" relationship. It might seem at first that altruistic love would be the fundamental principle in this case also, but the greater complexity of group relationships requires a correspondingly more complex principle of moral interaction. Let us examine more closely what is involved.

Any society or social group is determined by two things: first, the personal qualities of the individuals who make up the collectivity; and, second, the formal structure of the group. Society = people (individuals) + structure. Social structures arise from implicit and explicit agreements and conventions according to which the collectivity is seen to have certain goals and certain norms. Goals determine the purposes of group activity and norms establish the rules that govern group activity in the pursuit of group goals.

In particular, social structures define a certain number of roles or functions which an individual may play in the pursuit of group goals. Whenever an individual plays a specific role in the group, he must conform to the norms established by the group for that role; he is not free to perform the function according to his strictly personal proclivities alone. Also, just being a member of the group is in itself a role, and there are (explicit or implicit) general group norms that apply to all group members. Thus, the total effect of group structures is to establish the group as a social organism having a collective personality (or group identity) and with the individuals as its cells.

Practically speaking, the existence of group structures and norms means that relationships within the context of a given group have at least three components:

(1) a personal component in which two group members relate purely in terms of their personal identities, independently of group norms and goals;

(2) a functional component in which two group members relate on the basis of their respective roles within the group;

(3) a global component which derives from the relationship each group member has to the group as a whole.

Altruistic love and reciprocal friendship would be the natural basis of the purely personal component of a group relation. However, the functional and global aspects of group relations bring into play other principles, which are primarily related to the concept of social (rather than purely individual) justice. Social justice involves, on the one hand, *rights*, meaning that the group norms recognize what an individual is allowed to do in a given context, and, on the other hand, *obligations*, which determine what the individual is required to do in the given context. Social justice is established whenever both rights and obligations are respected and observed by everyone.

Of course, in any given case, and depending on the nature of group norms and goals, social justice may have either much or little to do with the authentic justice described in sections 2 and 3 above, which was defined as the knowledge and implementation of what is appropriate to the satisfaction of legitimate human needs and the development of human spiritual potential. A given social system therefore has a moral value, which is greater or lesser depending on the degree to which the justice of the system approximates authentic justice. A social system that approximates authentic justice to a greater degree than another is said to be a "more just" system than the other. Thus, in the same way that we strive to approximate pure altruistic love in our individual relations, we should strive that our social systems approximate pure justice to the greatest possible degree.

The Bahá'í Writings stress that the worst possible social configuration is anarchy—the total absence of any social order whatsoever—because such a situation leads eventually (usually quite quickly) to rampant powerseeking and the complete domination of the less powerful by the more powerful. Anarchy is, so to speak, a process of negative natural selection in which the very worst elements of society and of human nature come to the fore. For instance, anyone who tries to practice altruistic love in such a system will be quickly victimized, enslaved, or killed. He may maintain his own moral integrity, but his moral superiority will have no effect on the system itself, nor will it guarantee his physical survival.

In other words, order itself has a positive moral value, however imperfect a particular system may be when compared with other possible systems. However, once an order is established, it is the moral duty of every member of the society to strive to increase the justness of that order. We thus have a first principle of group relations:

In group relations, we should always act in such a way as to increase the justness of the group structure.

The problem with this principle, in its present form, is that it has logical content but no substantive content. It does not tell us what are the features of a social order that may serve to render it more just than it is. This brings us to the question of the moral value of the purposes and norms of a society: what should be the goal of a society and how should a just goal be justly pursued?

The commonly received answer to this question is that society exists primarily as a market place, as an arena for economic activity. Crudely put, the principle of a market society is that whatever helps the economy is good and whatever hinders it is bad. It then follows that if certain social norms and structures are painful or oppressive to a segment of the population, but are nonetheless good for the economy, then the painful and oppressive features of the system must be endured. This degree of unjustness in the system represents "the price we pay" to have a healthy economy that will presumably be of more long term benefit than a less healthy economy based on a more just system of norms and values.

In any event, the usual assumption is that there is an unavoidable, intrinsic opposition between the good of the individual and the good of society as a whole. A consequence of this view is that most social systems are seen as a compromise in which a certain degree of individual self-realization must be sacrificed for the establishment of the social order.

Authentic morality, and the Bahá'í Writings in particular, challenge and refute this conception of the social order. Authentic morality holds that the underlying purpose of any social order is or should be to create a social environment which maximizes the spiritual growth and development of each member of the society. In other words, the moral value of a social order is precisely measured by the degree to which it facilitates the development of human spiritual potential. In this view, all other social goals and purposes, including economic development, are secondary, though perhaps legitimate in themselves:

> . . . the object of life to a Bahá'í is to promote the oneness of mankind. The whole object of our lives is bound up with the lives of all human beings; not a personal salvation we are seeking, but a universal one. . . . Our aim is to produce a world civilization which will in turn react on the character of the individual.[24]

Thus, the principle that guides us in the elaboration of social structures is unity: those social structures that favor cooperation, mutuality, and reciprocity are good, and those that favor competition, powerseeking, and conflict are bad. We have a moral duty to strive to replace bad or defective social structures with good or better ones.

However, the process of change must also be just, because otherwise conflict and anarchy will ensue and the ultimate result will be a worse system, however good the initial intentions of the reformers. There must be a harmony of means and ends: moral ends cannot be obtained by unjust means.

Authentic unity is a unity in diversity, which respects and encourages all creative and legitimate differences, not a uniformity that seeks to suppress individual difference. Indeed, it is not individual differences themselves that lead to conflict and competition, but rather a lack of tolerance towards (love for) such differences, which betrays our underlying insecurity and consequent will to dominate the other.

---

24. Ruḥíyyih Khánúm, "To the Bahá'í Youth," *Bahá'í News*, no. 231 (May 1950): p. 6.

A somewhat subtle but crucial logical distinction must be made here. It is not social structures but individuals who compete, seek power, or engage in conflictual behavior towards each other. The very existence of morality and moral questions depends upon the existence of individual free will. Otherwise, we could not be held responsible for our actions any more than a computer could be blamed for executing its program. Thus, in the final analysis, all questions of morality pertain to the individual in one way or another. As Shoghi Effendi has said: "Ultimately all the battle of life is within the individual. No amount of organization can solve the inner problems or produce or prevent, as the case may be, victory or failure at a crucial moment."[25]

However, it is equally clear that the moral quality (justness or unjustness) of social structures has a powerful influence on individual moral choice. In the context of an overwhelmingly negative social environment, a few moral heroes will undoubtedly persist in pursuing moral authenticity, but the vast majority will be dragged down by negative influences instead of rising above them.

Thus, the moral value (positive or negative) of a social structure is measured ultimately by the influence it has on individual moral behavior. But we have already established that the principle governing individual human relations is altruistic love. Hence the obvious conclusion: *the justness or unjustness of a social order is reflected in the degree to which that order is favorable or unfavorable to the flourishing of altruistic love between its individual members.*

So when we say, as we have above, that there is no intrinsic conflict between the authentic individual good and the authentic social good, we are saying that a just social order is possible. In other words: *There exist social structures which encourage and permit, and in no wise discourage or limit, the flourishing of altruistic love between individuals.* Such a social order will be characterized by authentic justice and authentic love—hence by true and enduring unity, recalling again our fundamental equation: unity = justice + love. We are now ready

---

25. On behalf of Shoghi Effendi, from a letter dated December 18, 1943, to an inidividual believer, in *Living the Life: A Compilation*, p. 20.

to formulate our full principle governing the moral relationship between an individual and a social group:

> *With respect to society or a social group, we should always act so as to increase the authentic unity of the collectivity.*

Though succinctly stated, this principle is pregnant with meaning. Recalling the three components of group relations (personal, functional, and global), it means that, with respect to personal relationships within the group, we continue to act on the principle of altruistic love and, with respect to the functional and global components, we act to increase the justness of the system. In particular, if the goals and norms of the group are morally legitimate (which does not mean they are perfect), then we will show our support for the society by respecting socially established rights and accomplishing our socially required duties, whether specifically with regard to our role within the group or generally with regard to our relationship with the group as a whole.

What if either the goals or norms of a group are not morally legitimate? Then, of course we should not be a member of such a group. Indeed, we should strive to have no relationship with it whatsoever. As Bahá'u'lláh has said: "Walk not with the ungodly and seek not fellowship with him, for such companionship turneth the radiance of the heart into infernal fire."[26]

What if we have no choice but to be a part of a morally illegitimate society? Then we must still act as best we can to increase the justness of the social order and show forth altruistic love in our personal relationships. However, while recognizing that such an unjust order may be morally preferable to anarchy (see pp. 92–93), we cannot compromise our moral authenticity to satisfy truly immoral obligations such an order may impose upon us. We can of course try to avoid a situation which would require us to break openly with the established authority. Such avoidance action is not cowardice but

---

26. Bahá'u'lláh, *The Hidden Words*, Persian, no. 57.

wisdom and moderation in the pursuit of unity. But when and if such a situation is forced upon us (e.g., we are required by social authority to act cruelly or unjustly towards another), then we have no choice but to refuse and to accept the social consequences of such a refusal. We then become a true martyr (true because we have not actively sought to provoke the persecution heaped upon us).

Some moral philosophers have sincerely argued that the threat of extreme social sanctions, such as torture, unjust imprisonment, or death, changes the overall moral equation and thereby relieves the individual of all moral responsibility if he acts immorally when under this kind of duress. If, for example, I am threatened with death as a consequence of a refusal to act immorally on behalf of an unjust social authority, then why should I not preserve my life so as not to deprive my wife and children of my support? Maybe someone else will commit the immoral act anyway and I will have sacrificed my life for no good reason (except, some would say, my stubborn moral pride).

From the point of view of authentic morality, the fault in this argument can be clearly seen as soon as one reflects that the person who survives by deliberately perpetrating an act he knows and judges to be immoral is not the same as the person who existed before the act in question was committed. The *apparent* choice involved in the dilemma of "save your life by committing this one act under duress or die without having really changed anything" is no choice at all. You literally *cannot* preserve the person you currently are if you consciously perpetrate an immoral act. As soon as the act is committed, the moral self regresses (at least temporarily) to a lesser self which survives in your place. Thus, the only real choice in such a situation is between the survival of the authentic, moral self or the temporary physical survival of the body (which will eventually die in any case).[27]

---

27. Such dramatic moral situations raise in a particularly sharp way the fundamental question of life after death and the immortal existence of the soul. Our treatment here shows that the logic of authentic morality allows us to determine the correct principle—preservation of the authentic self—without necessarily resolving the question of immortal life. Let us stress, however, that our logic will be acceptable only to someone who adopts

Of course, it is one thing to engage in all of these abstract arguments and analyses and quite another to have the courage actually to make such a morally authentic choice when in extreme circumstances. Indeed, everyone agrees that the existence of social duress considerably diminishes moral responsibility (but without entirely eliminating it as we have seen). In other words, there is certainly an objective moral difference between someone who perpetrates an immoral act for purely selfish ends under normal circumstances and one who perpetrates the same act only under extreme duress. But recognizing this difference does not change the objective truth of the moral equation which dictates that we cannot maintain the same level of moral authenticity while deliberately perpetrating a morally reprehensible act.

Most people live their lives without ever facing such dramatic dilemmas as having to choose between moral authenticity and the preservation of physical life. Nevertheless, all human being are daily faced with moral choices of various magnitudes, and everyone's moral courage is tested sooner or later. For example, the simple act of willingly incurring the rejection and disapproval of one's friends rather than compromising one's moral principles can take immense courage, especially if one must continue to live daily in the same milieu or within the same social system as do the friends in question.

But more importantly, it is not sufficient for moral authenticity that we refrain from moral compromise and avoid thereby becoming a cause of disunity or injustice in our group relations. Authentic morality requires that we become proactive *unifiers*—that we actively and dynamically seek to facilitate a continual increase in the degree of unity of those morally legitimate groups of which we are a mem-

---

the basic assumptions of authentic morality (in particular, the notion of the existence of the individual, nonmaterial soul with its inherent capacities of consciousness, knowledge, love, and will), and these assumptions imply, however indirectly, that the soul is indeed immortal. Thus, a person with a strong disbelief in life after death is probably not very likely to accept the system of authentic morality in the first place, though there could of course be exceptions. It is nonetheless logically significant that acceptance of the soul's immortality is in no wise a precondition to adopting the system of authentic morality.

ber. Social participation is thus an important and irreplaceable aspect of the process of authentic moral development. The moral challenge of overcoming injustice and disunity in group relations presents unique opportunities for spiritual growth that do not occur within the context of purely individual, one-to-one relations.

7. The Self's Relationship with the Self

There is no doubt that consciousness is the most fundamental capacity and defining attribute of the human being. Our self-awareness creates an inner world of purely personal and subjective states, sensations, thoughts, and feelings to which only we have direct access. Of course, these inner states and sensations, though subjective in themselves, may well be responses to our encounter with various external stimuli.

You and I each presume that there is a similarity between our respective inner responses to similar stimuli. We base this presumption (in general quite reasonably) on two observable similarities: the similarity of our *protocols*, our descriptions of the inner sensations themselves, and the similarity of our observable responses to similar stimuli. But beyond this, we have absolutely no way of knowing whether your inner experience of, say the color red, is the same as my inner experience of that color. We can only observe that we both tend to classify the same objects as red or not red, and that your description of your experience of the beauty of a red rose seems to confirm my own and to coincide with it.

But suppose, for example, that in truth I experience as red what you call the color green and experience as green what you call the color red. How would we ever know this? We would both continue to classify the same objects as red or not red, and our protocols might even be the same if I happen to feel about what I call red the same way you feel about green. The point is that only I have access to *my* inner states and only you have access to yours. Our respective behaviors and protocols are equally observable by both of us, but these data are at least once removed from the respective inner states that give rise to them.

Thus, from the point of view of my individual self, my experience of reality constitutes a *hierarchy of accessibility*. At the first level of the hierarchy is my subjectivity, which consists of those data to which I have immediate (unmediated) and privileged access; immediate because my access to these states does not depend on anyone else's protocol or behavior, and privileged because no one else has such access to these data. The data that give rise to this first level of experience are part of *subjective reality*, i.e., that portion of reality which is wholly internal to one or more human subjects.

The second level of the hierarchy consists of those data to which all normally endowed human subjects have equal, independent, and direct access. These data consist of concrete, physical objects that can be perceived by the external senses of any normally endowed human being. They comprise *observable* (or *concrete*) *reality*, and form a part of *objective reality*, i.e., that portion of reality which is wholly external to any human subjectivity.

Of course, I do not have purely direct access to concrete physical objects. I have direct access only to the internal subjective sensations and states that occur as a result of my encounter with these objects. However, I do have direct access to these data in the precise sense that my ability to perceive them is inherent in my own nature, and I have independent access because such perception does not depend on the protocol or the behavior of any other human subject. In other words, the only subjectivity that mediates to me the knowledge of observable reality is my own.

Notice that an individual observer may have temporary privileged access to a given concrete object, because he may be observing the object from a superior position with respect to other observers. For example, if I am looking at a cell through a microscope, I am in a better position to observe this phenomenon that you are. But, in principle, you may also subsequently look at the object through the microscope and thus gain the same access as I now have.

However, this equality of access to concrete data is an equality-in-principle, which may not always be realized in practice (suppose I own the microscope and won't let you look through it). It is therefore important to realize that, in practice, you can "verify" or validate my observation only to the degree that you are capable of assuming and willing to assume my position of observation (standpoint) with respect to the object in question.

Finally, there is *invisible reality*, which consists of those objective data to which we have only indirect access. Invisible reality is the nonobservable portion of objective reality. It comprises entities and forces that cannot be perceived by the physical senses but whose existence can be deduced from the way observable reality behaves. For example, we cannot perceive the invisible force of gravity itself, but we can observe the fact that unsupported objects all fall in a downward direction, and this without any observable reason. We therefore infer or deduce that the cause of this observed behavior is the action of an unobservable force called gravity.

Invisible entities may be physical forces, like gravity or magnetism, or they may be nonphysical (spiritual) entities, such as the mind, the soul, or the force of altruistic love between two people. Our vision of the structure of invisible reality is therefore *conceived* by a creative act of the mind, rather than *perceived* by the external senses, as in the case of concrete reality. This does not mean that invisible reality is any less objective than observable reality, only that our access to it is less direct.

To complete our terminology, we define *abstract reality* as that portion of total reality which cannot be perceived by the external senses. Abstract reality is therefore comprised of subjective reality (including our own subjectivity) and the invisible portion of objective reality. In other words, abstract reality is everything except concrete reality. It therefore involves two different categories of accessibility.

We can thus say, with deliberate oversimplification, that we primarily feel our own subjective reality, that we primarily perceive concrete reality, and that we primarily conceive abstract reality (or at least that portion of it outside our own subjectivity). But the important point is that these processes of feeling, perceiving, and conceiving are interrelated in such a way that we cannot really separate out the components one from the other. Rather, we experience reality as a seamless whole that we are simultaneously and continuously feeling, perceiving, and conceiving. Indeed, it often takes a tremendous effort of will and a tremendous degree of self-insight to realize that a given perception, let us say of an ideal beloved, is arising primarily from our own subjectivity rather than from the objective qualities or characteristics of the person who is the object of our love.

But more fundamentally, the human being is not just a feeling and perceiving machine that generates conceptions and behavior in response to external stimuli. From the moment the human soul or self exists, it has an intrinsic structure. From the very beginning of our life we *are* something and we *bring* something to our encounters with reality. This is the intrinsic value of the human being, which is both universal and inherent in God-created human nature. There are, of course, individual differences, but these differences take place within certain limits and within the context of certain overall similarities that define universal human nature—what is common to all human beings. This universal human nature is represented by the capacities of consciousness, thought, feeling, and will that we have discussed above in chapter 2.

Our intrinsic value is thus determined by our capacities, which define what we are, and our limitations, which define what we are not. Our capacities define the extent of the self, and our limitations define the boundary of the self. Some of our limitations are absolute and permanent (no human will ever become God) and some are relative and temporary (the child has limits he will one day overcome and surpass). Limitations of the latter kind depend on our abilities (see chapter 2 above), i.e., the extent to which we have currently actualized our inherent capacities.

But now we come to the important point: we do not have the spontaneous knowledge of the extent of our capacities (or even our abilities) or of the nature of our limitations (whether temporary or permanent), any more that we have the spontaneous knowledge of the structure of objective reality. Initially, the self—our self—is just as much a mystery as any other aspect of reality. Moreover, for each individual, there are certain aspects of the self that can only be known by that self, which is the only self having access to the subjective states of that self.

Or put it another way: you can only have the same knowledge of a given reality as I if you are capable of assuming and willing to assume the same position as I with regard to that reality. But you *cannot*, now or ever, assume the position that I have with regard to the reality of my self.

Thus, the reflexive relationship of the self to the self is unique among all relationships the self has. This uniqueness is due to the fact that the self has privileged access to certain data about itself, namely its internal, subjective states. We can therefore enunciate the basic principle governing the relationship of the self with itself:

> *In our relationship with our own self, we should always act so as to increase our knowledge of the authentic reality of the self. This means accurate knowledge both of our capacities and abilities on one hand, and of our (permanent and temporary) limitations on the other.*

It is immediately clear, in a general way, why an increase in self-knowledge is a useful thing, but why is increasing self-knowledge a *moral* principle? What relation does it have to moral values?

To answer this question, we must recall the basic parameters of authentic morality outlined in the foregoing development. Morality is the pursuit of authentic relationships. Such relationships are established and maintained by the proper development of our fundamental capacities of mind, heart, and will, which results in an increase in autonomy and well-being. Our autonomy derives from authentic knowledge of reality, including in particular the law of causality, and our well-being results from the effective implementation of this knowledge to obtain the authentic satisfaction of legitimate human needs, both for ourselves and others. Finally, the process of developing our intrinsic capacities involves interactions—an ongoing dialogue between ourselves and reality, in which the structure of reality imposes certain conditions upon us that then force us to respond in some manner, leading to a further step in the dialogue.

Thus, the interaction is the basic unit of moral development, and any given interaction involves an encounter between the inner structure of the self, on one hand, and the structure of some portion of reality on the other. An interaction is a challenge, and a given challenge can be perceived as either an opportunity for growth or a threat to the self, depending on the intensity of the challenge and the inner resources we can summon up to meet the challenge. Thus, knowledge of the authentic self—its capacities, abilities, and limitations—is fully one half of the moral equation. Unless we have some accurate idea of what we actually bring to the challenges of life, we cannot succeed in the process of moral development, no matter how well we may comprehend the structure of, say, objective concrete reality (i.e., possess what is usually called scientific knowledge of material reality).

Suppose, for example, that I am sincerely and consciously striving to implement the principle of altruistic love in my relationships with others, and you behave towards me in some irritating or unjust manner (perhaps you criticize me unfairly or even insult and berate me). Your behavior represents a genuine challenge to my ability to generate an authentic love response instead of a power response. Suppose, now, that I know myself well enough to realize that I am being challenged beyond the limits of the present development of my capacities. I feel my anger, irritation, and desire for revenge growing, and I know that if we continue in this configuration much longer, I will not be able to control myself. I may explode in anger or deliberately sabotage your life—tell a lie about you or seek to destroy your image in the eyes of others.

Knowing as I do that such undesirable behavior on my part is the likely—indeed inevitable—outcome of a continuation of the present configuration of our relationship, I have only two choices. I must either temporarily withdraw and de-intensify our interaction, or else find some way to get you to change your behavior towards me. (Perhaps just talking to you openly and frankly, and pointing out to you the nature of your behavior, will be enough.)

Now suppose that I am presented with the same challenge, but am lacking in adequate self-knowledge. Then, on the one hand, I may generate a *hypocritical response* in which I pretend to be untouched by your behavior but am really seething with anger. More precisely, suppose I have an image of myself as a loving person who is able to implement the principle of altruistic love at a very high level, but that this self-image is false: I have not yet developed the ability to generate a love response in this situation. However, since I do not correctly perceive my limitations, I may pretend to act in a loving manner even though it is a performance (for myself as much as for others). I am *projecting the ideal (wished-for) reality onto the actual reality*. I have an idealized, unrealistic self-image which I strive to actualize by acting *as if* this imagined self was the real or actual self.

On the other hand, I may generate a *defensive response*, in which I try to deny the reality of my limitations and attribute my failure to generate the hoped-for response to a perceived threat arising from some feature of external reality beyond my control. Of course, your insulting behavior is no threat to my authentic self: your unfair criticism of me cannot subtract anything from what I really am, any more than your flattery (if forthcoming) can add to what I am. But your behavior is a genuine threat to my false self-image, which claims that I should not feel towards you the anger and resentment that I do in fact feel. Thus, I can maintain the false self-image only by denying the reality of my angry feelings or else justifying these feelings as a legitimate response to a genuine external threat (as if, for example, I were about to be convicted in court of a crime I did not commit and thus victimized by forces beyond my control).

In both these hypothetical cases the challenge is the same and the internal resources to meet the challenge are inadequate. But in one instance I have authentic knowledge of my limitations and can thus generate a growth-inducing response. For example, if I withdraw temporarily instead of giving in to the urge to use my power to punish you, I will have deliberately renounced the pursuit of power and thus taken a positive step forward in my moral development. In the other instance, without authentic self-knowledge, I may generate a response which constitutes a temporary regression in my moral development, since both hypocrisy and defensiveness are inimical to authentic love.

It is important to note that, in the context we have described, the response of a temporary withdrawal is not moral cowardice, nor does it represent abandonment of the pursuit of authentic self-development. In human relations, it might be compared to what, in military terms, is called a "strategic retreat," in which one withdraws temporarily to regroup and increase inner resources as a basis for a more effective advance in the future. Moreover, the very fact that we deliberately restrain ourselves from a power-based response that we were fully capable of producing constitutes, in itself, a high level of authentic striving for moral autonomy. Finally, realization of our limitations enables us to become more aware of our dependence on God which, as we have seen above, is one of the principles conducive to authentic moral development.

Besides being interesting in itself, this example serves to illustrate a fundamental principle of the process of moral development. Let us call it the *positive growth principle*:

Whether a given encounter with reality results in authentic moral growth or not depends primarily on the nature of our response to the challenge offered by the encounter and very little on the nature of the challenge itself.

The positive growth principle means that authentic moral development depends very little on the outward circumstances of our life. It means that, even in very difficult and trying conditions, it is usually possible to find a growth-inducing response. The positive growth principle is an expression of divine justice, because it signifies that the conditions for successful moral growth are in our own hands and not in the hands of others, or of circumstances beyond our control. We literally hold our spiritual destiny in the palm of our hand.

Notice that the positive growth principle does not hold for other areas of endeavor. Unfavorable circumstances beyond our control can easily frustrate our success in business, science, or art. If success in these areas is our primary goal in life, most of us are doomed to frustration and failure. But if we truly understand and diligently apply the principles of moral development in our life, we are guaranteed success regardless of the difficult conditions that life may put upon us.

Of course, the law of cause and effect is objective and applies in all areas of human life. But in the realm of the moral, we have a different relationship to the law of causality because we have control over our moral response to the circumstances of life, and this response constitutes the greater part of the cause necessary to produce an effect of increased moral development.

Thus, authentic self-knowledge is knowledge of the authentic self, its capacities and the current state of their development, and its limitations (whether relative and temporary or absolute and permanent). At any given stage of the moral development process, the current state of our self-knowledge is synthesized in a global self-image, which represents our conception of what we are. We try to actualize this self-image in all our relationships. But, to the degree that the self-image is fase, such actualization is impossible.

The self-image is part of the global inner model of reality discussed at the end of chapter 2. In order to understand more fully the moral implications of self-knowledge, we need to examine more closely the relationship between the self-image, the total inner model, and reality itself.

8. The Self-Image and the Inner Model

We begin our discussion by recalling the fundamental principle first encountered in chapter 1, section 7: human actions and motivations are determined not by reality but by our overall perception (view) of reality. This overall perception is based on our inner model of reality, which reflects the current state of the perceptions, conceptions, and emotional attitudes derived from the sum of all our interactions with reality until the present moment. (See the initial discussion of inner models in chapter 2, section 8) In particular, our inner model contains our internalized picture of the causality relationship (see section 4 above, p. 82 ff.).

Thus, to the degree that our inner model of reality accurately reflects the causality relationship between phenomena, our expectations about life will be realistic: what we expect to happen under given circumstances will usually happen in the manner we anticipate. In scientific terms, our inner model represents our "theory of life," which makes predictions about how things will behave under certain conditions (i.e., when certain hypotheses are satisfied). If expectations based upon our theory are realized in actual fact, then the correctness of the total theory is partially confirmed, and if not, then something is wrong with our model and we have a partial refutation of our theory.

We give a schematic representation of the relationship between the inner model and reality in the following diagram:

Relationship Between Inner Model and Reality

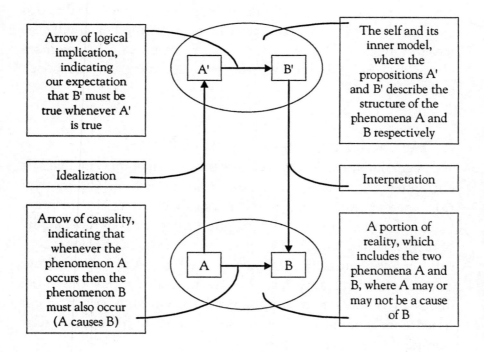

Fig. 3.1. Relationship between inner model and reality

Explanation of Diagram

By the mental process of idealization, we represent within our subjectivity (mind) the two observed (or conceived) phenomena A and B by two propositions A' and B' each of which describes the corresponding phenomenon as existing in the way we have perceived or conceived it. Our inner model will be correct if our idealization process has correctly identified and represented (reflected) the fundamental logical features of the phenomena A and B. If our model is in fact correct and if the phenomenon A does in fact cause the phenomenon B, then our proposition A' will logically imply B'. But if our formulation of propositions A' and B' is incorrect (our inner model is inaccurate), then A' may imply B' even if A does not cause B, or else A' may not imply B' even though A does in fact cause B. In either of the last two cases, our prediction or expectation, represented by the arrow of interpretation, will not be realized. But, if our inner model is accurate, and if A does in fact cause B, then our expectation (prediction) will be realized, and we can go from A to B either directly (experimentation) or else by the sequence idealization–implication–interpretation (reason).

* * *

Thus, if what we expect to happen does not happen, it is a first indication that our inner model may be faulty or inadequate. It is faulty to the degree that it reflects an incorrect picture of reality and inadequate to the degree that it reflects a partial picture of reality. Faults derive from self-generated or other-generated distortions of our inner model (see chapter 2, section 8, p. 57 ff) whereas inadequacies derive from the incompleteness of our information about reality.

Our inner model is thus a mosaic of true and false, of accuracy and distortion, of exactness and vagueness. But we of course experience our inner model not as a mosaic but as a seamless whole, because for us our model *is* (our view of) reality. We thus do not usually have direct insight into the incongruities between our model and reality, because as soon as we become aware of such incongruities our inner model changes. For example, I will not usually view an object as green while knowing it is red. When I truly know that it is red I will then begin to view it as red.

Given that our inner states are more directly accessible to us than any objective phenomenon (especially an abstract one), generating an accurate inner model (correct reason) allows us to achieve a higher level of autonomy than does continual resort to the trial-and-error of direct experimentation. But of course a certain amount of experimentation (experience) will be necessary in order to construct the inner model in the first place. Thus, as we have already seen in our discussion of interactions, the process of building an (accurate) inner model is a dialogue between ourselves and reality involving encounters (both spontaneous and deliberate) with reality and our active, inner responses to these encounters.

In particular, the process of generating our inner model involves internal encounters of the self with the self, as well as the sharing of protocol with other human subjects (intersubjective verification). We thus make inner models not only of portions of objective reality but also of subjective reality including our own self. This inner model of the self is what we have called the *self-image*. It constitutes the overall internal conception we have of our capacities, limitations, and worth—both intrinsically and in relation to others.

The self-image is fundamental to the inner model because it is involved to some extent in virtually every encounter with any portion of reality. I may be able to live a long and happy life with a faulty inner model of the Amazonian jungle or of the penguins in Antarctica, especially if I never actually encounter these phenomena. But a faulty perception of my own capacities and limitations is almost bound to cause considerable dysfunction and diminished autonomy at some point in my development.

Not only is the self-image so central, it is also the most fragile, value-sensitive aspect of our inner model. In chapter 1, we have examined in detail how false, but socially predominant, value notions such as individualism or collectivism can contribute to the creation of a false self-image that hides from us the objective reality of our own God-given intrinsic value. Indeed, stressing the importance of self-knowledge, Bahá'u'lláh counsels that we should "gain a true knowledge of your own selves—a knowledge which is the same as the comprehension of Mine own Being,"[28] and, in another passage, states that "'He hath known God who hath known himself.'"[29]

Our self-image thus represents our expectations about ourselves—of how we (the reality of the self) will behave under certain conditions and of how others will act towards us. When these expectations are not met, we have the first indication that our self-image may be distorted (faulty or inadequate).

To say that our self-image is distorted means that it does not correspond to reality, the reality that is within us. Perhaps we have an exaggerated image of ourselves, believing we have talents and abilities we lack in reality. We may, at the same time and in other ways, underestimate ourselves, carrying an unrealistically negative concept of our capacities.

In any case, to the degree that our self-concept is false we will experience unpleasant tensions and difficulties as we become involved in various life situations. The false or unrealistic parts of our self-image will be implicitly judged by our encounter with reality. We will sense this and begin to perceive, at first vaguely and uncomfortably but then more sharply, that something is wrong. Even though this feedback information from reality may be from neutral sources and devoid of any value-judgmental quality, we may nevertheless perceive it as a threat or even an attack. If the feedback is not neutral but comes, say, in the form of blatantly negative criticism from others, our sense of being threatened will certainly be much greater.

Moreover, we will perceive the source of these threats as being somewhere outside ourselves. It will not naturally occur to us that the source lies rather within ourselves in the form of an illusory and unrealistic self-concept. Therefore, our instinctive reaction to the negative feedback information will be to resist, to defend our self-image and to strive to maintain it.

---

28. Bahá'u'lláh, *Gleanings*, pp. 326–327.
29. Ibid., p. 178.

In defending our self-image, we believe we are defending our selves because we do not view ourselves as a mosaic of true and false, real and unreal. We see only the seamless, undifferentiated whole of "I" or "me." The result is that we begin to bind up more and more of our mental energy in the defense of our self-image. We confuse egotistic pride, which is our attachment to our limited and distorted self-concept, with self-respect and honor, which are expressions of the deep spiritual truth that we are created in the image of God with an intrinsic value given by Him and without any essentially evil or sinful part.

The "binding energy" involved in our defense of our self-concept is frequently experienced as various negative emotions like fear, rage, jealousy, or aggressiveness. These emotions are all expressions of our attempt to locate the source of our irritation outside ourselves in objective, external reality. We are also liable to experience considerable anxiety as we cling more and more desperately to whatever false part of ourselves we cannot relinquish. Clearly, the greater the pathology of our self-image and the greater our attachment to it, the stronger will be our sense of being threatened and attacked, and the greater will be the amount of inner energy necessary to maintain and defend the false part of our self-image.

At this point, an increase in self-knowledge will be represented by some insight into ourselves which enables us to discard a false part of our self-image. This act of self-knowledge is the first stage involved in taking a step forward in the process of spiritual growth. Such an increment in self-knowledge has one immediate consequence: it instantly releases that part of our mental energy which was previously bound up in defending and maintaining the false self-concept. The release of this binding energy is most usually experienced as an extremely positive emotion, a sense of exhilaration and liberation. It is love. We have a truer picture of our real (and therefore God-created) selves, and we have a new reservoir of energy which is now freed for its God-intended use in the form of service to others.

Following this release of energy will be an increase in courage. We have more courage partly because we have more knowledge of reality and have therefore succeeded in reducing, however slightly the vastness of what is unknown and hence potentially threatening to us. We also have more courage because we have more energy to deal with whatever unforeseen difficulties may lie ahead. This new increment of courage constitutes an increase in faith.

Courage generates within us *intentionality*, i.e., the willingness and the desire to act. We want to act because we are anxious to exper-ience the sense of increased mastery that will come from dealing with life situations which previously appeared difficult or impossible but which now seem challenging and interesting. And we are also eager to seek new challenges, to use our new knowledge and energy in circumstances we would have previously avoided. And, most importantly, we have an intense desire to share with others, to serve them and to be an instrument, to whatever possible extent, in the process of their spiritual growth and development.

Finally, this intentionality, this new motivation, expresses itself in concrete action. Until now everything has taken place internally, in the inner recesses of our psyche. No external observer could possibly know that anything significant has transpired. But when we began to act, the reality of this inner process is dramatized. Action, then, is the dramatization of intentionality and therefore of knowledge, faith, and love. It is the visible, observable concomitant of the invisible process that has occurred within us.

We have taken a step forward in our spiritual development. We have increased our moral autonomy; we have moved from one level to another. However small the step may be, however minimal the difference between the old level of functioning and the new, a definite transition has taken place.

Whenever we act, we affect not only ourselves but also our physical and social environment. Our action thereby evokes a reaction from others. This reaction is, of course, just a form of the feedback information mentioned above. But the difference is that our action has now been the result of a conscious and deliberate process. We know why we acted the way we did. Thus, we will perceive the reaction in a different way, even if it is negative (our good intentions certainly do not guarantee that the reaction will be positive). We will welcome the reaction because it will help us evaluate our actions. In short the reaction to our actions will give us new knowledge, new self-insight. In this way, the cycle starts again and the process of taking another step along the path of moral development is repeated. We represent this process by the following diagram:

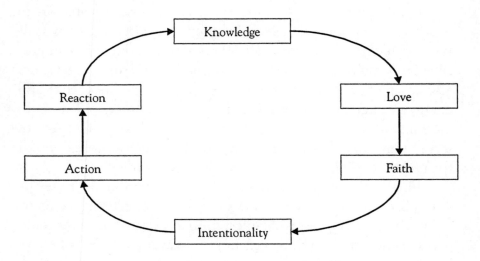

Fig. 3.2. The "virtuous cycle" of authentic spiritual growth

Notice how an increase in autonomy and well-being is related to an increase in self-knowledge. Our egotistic and narcissistic attachment to our false self-image limits our autonomy, impelling us on an impossible and potentially endless quest to fulfill the expectations of our vainly conceived self-concept. Indeed, such enslavement to a false self-concept is the very antithesis of the autonomy that is the natural result of authentic self-knowledge and consequent self-mastery. The liberation of the energy previously bound up in the defense of a false self-concept increases our capacity for action and thus our freedom.

Confrontation with, and knowledge of, the authentic self also frees us from the negative emotions of envy, jealousy, anxiety, and rage that are involved in the defense of a false self-concept. Liberation from the vice of these negative emotions constitutes, in itself, a considerable increase in well-being, and is also the first step towards opening up the heart to the experience of the powerful positive emotions of joy and altruistic love.

There is likewise an extremely close connection between knowledge of the authentic self and knowledge of God and our dependency on Him. Knowledge of our authentic capacities is knowledge of the image of God within us, and knowledge of our limitations makes us aware of all the ways we need God's help in the pursuit of authentic relationships.

More generally, there is a resonance and mutual reinforcement among the principles that underlie each of the categories of interaction of the self. Authentic development along any one of these lines will naturally and inevitably lead to development along the others. Thus, even though it is practically useful to examine the specific moral principles underlying each category of interaction, we should constantly keep in mind that moral and spiritual development is a thoroughly integrated and coherent process. For a more detailed development of the logic of the virtuous cycle, see appendix III on pp. 143–151.

9. Other Categories of Interaction

The respective relationships of the self to God, to the self, to other individuals, and to society constitute the categories of interactions that are the most fundamental to the process of authentic moral development. However, all our interactions with whatever aspect of reality have some degree of significance for our moral development, and so we should nonetheless examine, if only briefly and in summary fashion, the principles relating to these other categories.

The principles of authentic morality imply that we should, in general, treat animals and other life forms with kindness and respect.

Exceptions are those animals, such as poisonous snakes or sharks, which are dangerous to humans. But even these categories of animals should not be treated with gratuitous cruelty, only with the force necessary to defend ourselves effectively from them.

Establishing an authentic relationship with other life forms can be seen as an appropriate balance between two possible extremes. One extreme would put all life forms on an equal basis and claim, for example, that animals have the same rights and prerogatives as humans. According to this view, we should seek to establish a perfectly symmetrical relationship with animals just as we strive to do with other human beings. This view lacks authenticity because it contradicts the fact that reality is structured as an objective value hierarchy in which humans are superior (more valuable) than other life forms (just as God is superior to humans). It is therefore unjust (inauthentic) to give the same value to a snake or a cat that we give to, say, a human infant. Of course, as long as we are not forced to choose between the two, we can treat both humans and animals with unmitigated kindness. But, when forced to choose, we must unhesitatingly give priority to humans over lower life forms.

The other extreme would be to take our superiority over other life forms as a license to treat them with disrespect and cruelty. If we humans are indeed superior to other forms of life, then we must demonstrate this superiority by treating them with care and love—the same way God demonstrates His superiority over us. Indeed, one of the aspects of superior value is superior power, but the fact that we *can* destroy and mistreat does not mean we are obliged to do so. Again, God has absolute power over us and could destroy us all if He chose to do so. Just as He refrains from misusing His power over us, we must refrain from misusing our power over lower forms of life.

The modern science of ecology has demonstrated conclusively that all living systems are interrelated. Thus, both the similarities and the differences between humans and other life forms must be taken into account if we are to relate authentically to our biological environment.

Our interactions with inanimate, material objects also have implications for authentic morality. The tendency in modern society is to deal with such objects primarily on the basis of attachment and possession, which binds us to these objects. In seeking to possess objects of material wealth, we may thus become enslaved by them: we make these material objects into ends for which we then sacrifice higher values. The ultimate absurdity is a territorial war, in which humans, the highest value in creation, kill each other over territory, which is essentially dirt, one of the lowest values in creation.

Any value system that sacrifices spiritual values for material ends is a form of *materialism*, and is morally inauthentic. The principle that governs our authentic relationship with material objects is therefore the *principle of appropriate use*. In general, this means that we use lower, material values to obtain higher, spiritual values (e.g., using objects of art to create an environment of beauty in the home). Thus, I may well own a computer or an automobile in order to facilitate communication and transportation in the pursuit of various legitimate spiritual goals. But if I cherish the possession of an automobile to the extent of making it an end itself, or if I spend much time playing computer games rather than developing my capacity for authentic human relations, then I have sacrificed a higher value for a lower one and thus misused these material objects.

It is therefore not the mere fact of the legal ownership of a material object that constitutes materialism. Such ownership can be seen as a useful social convention that helps determine who has legitimate access to the appropriate use of the object in question. It is the inner, spiritual attitude of attachment and possession that is morally inauthentic.

The temptation to materialism often derives from our tendency to invest material objects with a symbolic meaning. For example, if I consider my material possessions as a symbol of power, status, or sexual attractiveness, I may succumb to the illusion that such material ownership augments my human value. This illusion is the antithesis of the recognition of intrinsic value, which is the very basis of authentic morality.

The principle of appropriate use can also be applied to the way we treat our own bodies (although the body is, of course, a life form). If we want our body to serve spiritual purposes, then we should strive to keep it clean and healthy so that it functions well. This implies eating nutritious food in appropriate amounts, regular exercise, adequate sleep, and other healthful practices. The misuse of our bodies that corresponds analogously to the possession of and attachment to physical objects is the indulgence of bodily passions and appetites for their own sake, again making a means into an end. The point is that physical pleasure is not in itself morally inauthentic, but can become so if carried to excess and continually sought for its own sake.

We now turn to a consideration of our moral interaction with abstract reality, whether the subjective world of ideas or the objective world of unobservable forces and entities. We have already had occasion to appreciate the crucial importance for authentic morality of an accurate inner model of reality. A significant part of our inner model is comprised of the picture we have of unobservable reality—those objective phenomena to which we have only indirect access. Certain moral judgments we make and certain actions and attitudes we generate will depend on our view of unobservable reality (for example, on whether we know that God exists). *Thus, the principle of interaction with unobservable reality is that we should always act so as to maximize our knowledge of the structure of that reality.*

How is this done? The answer is: scientific method. The methods and techniques of science have been gradually generated and refined over a long period of time precisely to enable us to construct an accurate picture of the structure of unobservable reality. The point is that science and its methods have a moral or spiritual value and not just a practical or material value. With regard to the moral value of science, 'Abdu'l-Bahá has said, for example:

> All blessings are divine in origin, but none can be compared with this power of intellectual investigation and research, which is an eternal gift producing fruits of unending delight. Man is ever partaking of these fruits. All other blessings are temporary; this is an everlasting possession. . . . it is an eternal blessing and divine bestowal, the supreme gift of God to man.
>   . . . science or the attribute of scientific penetration is supernatural. . . .[30]

---

30. 'Abdu'l-Bahá, *Promulgation*, p. 50.

Of course, it is clearly impossible and indeed unnecessary that every human being should become a professional scientist. But a scientific approach and attitude towards life is accessible to every human being. Indeed, in the final analysis:

> Scientific method is the systematic, organized, directed, and conscious use of our various mental faculties in an effort to arrive at a coherent model of whatever phenomenon is being investigated.
>
> In a word, science is self-conscious common sense. Instead of relying on chance happenings or occasional experiences, one systematically invokes certain types of experiences. This is experimentation (the conscious use of experience). Instead of relying on naive reasoning, one formalizes hypotheses explicitly and formalizes the reasoning leading from hypothesis to conclusion. This is mathematics and logic (the conscious use of reason). Instead of relying on occasional flashes of insight, one systematically meditates on problems. This is reflection (the conscious use of intuition).[31]

In other words, God has ordained two sources of valid knowledge of the structure of reality. One source is constituted by the revelations of God through the Manifestations or great religious founders of history. This knowledge is preserved in the authenticated texts written or dictated by these Manifestations. The other source is science. Both science and religion are necessary to the construction of an accurate inner model of reality and thus to the successful pursuit of authentic moral development.[32]

Scientific method is also the basis of our authentic moral interaction with the world of ideas (the subjective portion of abstract reality). The (relative) moral value of an idea derives from its valid-

---

31. William S. Hatcher, *Logic and Logos*, p. 99.

32. See in particular 'Abdu'l-Bahá's comprehensive statement concerning the complementarity of revelation and science contained in His "Tablet of the Universe," pp. 4–7 (provisional translation, Haifa, 1995).

ity (the degree to which it approximates some portion of reality), on one hand, and its usefulness in contributing to the fulfillment of legitimate human needs, on the other. Generally speaking, valid and useful ideas are good and false and/or useless ideas are bad. Thus: *we should interact with ideas in such a way as to increase our ability to distinguish between good and bad ideas. Good ideas should be upheld and bad ideas discarded.*

An idea may be said to be *attractive* if it is perceived to be useful (it may or may not be useful in fact). Ideas that are highly attractive but false have the most negative moral value. It may be attractive for me to think that the world owes me a living and that I can act irresponsibly with no negative consequences. But since this idea is false, it will be very destructive to my moral authenticity if I accept the idea and act upon it.

Prejudices are frequent examples of false but attractive ideas. If I perceive myself as relatively unintelligent, then it may be attractive for me to think that all members of a racial group different from my own are less intelligent than I. But to succumb to this illusion will be very damaging to my moral authenticity.

Much more can be said about the relationship between authentic morality and the application of scientific method in our interactions with abstract reality. However, this would unduly lengthen our exposition, as well as perhaps serving to blur its focus to an unacceptable degree. We refer the interested reader to such works by the present author as *Logic and Logos,* in particular the essay "Myths, Models, and Mysticism" contained therein.[33]

Finally, let us look at general interactions, i.e., those in which no particular category of reality is dominant (see our scheme of interactions in chapter 2, section 4, pp. 44–45). The moral quality of these interactions depends primarily on what might be called our "general attitude" towards life, for example, whether we tend to be optimistic or pessimistic, fearful or bold, shy or self-confident. It is of course very difficult to separate such general attitudes from attitudes that are rationally based on concrete information. For example, I

---

33. Op. Cit.

may not be a fearful person in general, but in truly threatening circumstances, fear is a morally helpful and authentic response.

However, the modern world exhibits one pervasive, general attitude that is clearly morally inauthentic. This is a lack of openness to the full experience of life—an inability to see spiritual or moral meaning in simple things. Most of us have a limited number of specific activities that give us genuine pleasure: good times spent with friends, indulging our favorite foods, etc. But these pleasurable activities constitute only a small portion (say ten or fifteen percent) of our total interactions with life. We tend to regard our other, daily interactions as tedious, boring, or even actively unpleasant. We endure this daily round only by becoming insensitive to it—abstracting ourselves from it—and by looking forward to the activities we regard as truly pleasurable. Thus, we are truly alive only ten or fifteen percent of the time and we simply exist for the remainder.

To be morally authentic is to be fully alive at every moment of our existence, to be continually open to the experience of the new and of the other. *Thus, the principle that governs morally authentic general interactions is that we should always act so as to increase our consciousness and awareness of reality.* Moral development means a continual enlargement of consciousness and an increase in sensitivity and awareness.

To increase awareness and sensitivity is to open ourselves to an experience of the joy and meaning of life but also to its pain and suffering. To experience the other is to accept to share the pain of the other. This is undoubtedly one of the reasons why so many of the "recreational" activities of modern life, such as taking drugs or drinking alcohol, are devoted to decreasing consciousness and sensitivity rather than increasing them. We say that we need to "escape" from the painful realities of life.

Of course, pain and suffering are unpleasant, and no healthy, rational person deliberately seeks them out. Moreover, there is no virtue whatsoever in suffering for its own sake. However, for the successful pursuit of authentic relationships, autonomy, and well-being, a certain amount of suffering is necessary and inevitable, and we must be willing to accept this degree of suffering in order to achieve a stable, enduring joy and happiness. Thus, the morally authentic attitude is not that we seek to suffer, but that we accept to suffer whenever it proves necessary or unavoidable in the pursuit of moral authenticity.

In other words, we cannot increase our sensitivity and expand our consciousness by only opening ourselves selectively to that which brings us pleasure while systematically avoiding or suppressing whatever threatens to bring us pain. We must be open to the meaning of every aspect of life, and the truth is that the significance of some of life's aspects are revealed to us only through a certain amount of pain and suffering.

10. Authenticity, Autonomy, and Convergence

We have discussed the moral principles underlying each major category of interaction between the self and reality. Though more has been left unsaid than has been said, we nevertheless have before us the outlines of a morally authentic approach to the fundamental interactions of life. On this basis, we need now to articulate an integrated view of the rich and multifaceted notion of authenticity itself. We also need to gain a deeper understanding of the subtle relationship between individual autonomy and social order.

The word "authentic" connotes that which is real, genuine, trustworthy, integral, solid, or devoid of artifice. In attempting to achieve authenticity, there are two extremes which must be avoided. One is to regard as authentic everything that seems spontaneous, natural, and uncontrived. This is the Rousseauian, romantic notion that sees the source of inauthenticity in the rational side of our nature. It is a view that tends to equate rational thinking with calculation and calculation with indifference or egotistic self-interest. From this standpoint, achieving authenticity means to "let go" or jettison the rational self and allow the instinctive self to take over.

The problem with this view is that the rational self is just as much an authentic and innate part of human nature as is the emotional-instinctive self. Indeed, the Bahá'í Writings confirm the classical conception, deriving from Socrates, Plato, and Aristotle, that the rational self is higher than the instinctive self, and must predominate over the instinctive self if the pursuit of authenticity is to be successful:

> First and foremost among those favors, which the Almighty hath conferred upon man, is the gift of understanding. His purpose in conferring such a gift is none other except to enable His creature to know and recognize the one true God—exalted be His glory. This gift giveth man the power to discern the truth in all things, leadeth him to that which is right, and helpeth him to discover the secrets of creation. Next in rank, is the power of vision, the chief instrument whereby his understanding can function. The senses of hearing, of the heart, and the like, are similarly to be reckoned among the gifts with which the human body is endowed.[34]

Of course, to say that the mind is the highest faculty of the human being is not to say that the other faculties—e.g., will and emotion—are to be neglected or disparaged. Nor does it suggest that the mind cannot be misused and thereby become detrimental to authenticity. In fact, it is true of any human capacity that the greater its potential for good when properly used, the greater its potential for evil when misused.

The other unhealthy extreme is to think that we can achieve authenticity by the brute force of our will and intellect alone. The truth is that, unless aided by the power of God, we can achieve nothing, as Bahá'u'lláh has so clearly stated:

> Neither the candle nor the lamp can be lighted through their own unaided efforts, nor can it ever be possible for the mirror to free itself from its dross. It is clear and evident that until a fire is kindled the lamp will never be ignited, and unless dross is blot-

---

34. Bahá'u'lláh, *Gleanings*, p. 194.

ted out from the face of the mirror it can never represent the image of the sun nor reflect its light and glory.[35]

However, we should not hastily conclude from this principle that we can but passively await the descent of divine grace upon us. Indeed, God Himself has chosen to make the efficacy of His grace dependent upon the sincerity of our personal efforts:

> No matter how strong the measure of Divine grace, unless supplemented by personal, sustained and intelligent effort it cannot become fully effective and be of any real and abiding advantage.[36]

Thus, all success comes ultimately from God alone, but God requires that we demonstrate through action our purity of motive before He grants success. The fundamental prerequisite for authenticity is therefore sincerity of motivation, and our sincerity is proved by our actions and the quality of effort we deploy in the pursuit of authentic morality.

It would of course be much easier if moral authenticity could be achieved without such effort, but then the whole dimension of autonomy would be sacrificed. God has deliberately fashioned the structure of reality, and determined the parameters of our interactions with reality, in such wise that authentic well-being and moral autonomy are inseparable aspects of a single process. Authenticity leads to autonomy and autonomy to authenticity; each reinforces the other in continual reciprocity.

These principles all concern the individual, but what of the collectivity? Society cannot function without a certain minimal level of order and regularity, and this minimal functional level requires that everybody show respect for and obedience towards a basic set of rules and regulations that have been agreed upon in some generally recognized and accepted manner. How is this fundamental social

---

35. Ibid., p. 66.
36. Shoghi Effendi, quoted in *The Bahá'í Life*, p. 6.

exigency compatible with the autonomy of value choice that is so necessary to authenticity?

We have partly answered this question in our discussion in section 6 of the relationship between the self and society. We then saw that an essential element of individual authenticity is to act so as to increase the justness of social groups, and this attitude is incompatible with any kind of careless disregard for the legitimate rules of a given society, however unnecessary or trivial any such rule may appear to us personally.

Suppose, however, that every member of society is sincerely and respectfully pursuing moral authenticity, what guarantee do we have that people will not be sincerely led in different directions and end up making equally authentic but contradictory choices as autonomous moral agents? Is this not too great a risk to take? Can any society survive if it systematically encourages (or even allows) individual moral autonomy?

Down through history, most political, social, and religious leaders seemed to have given, in the last analysis, a strong negative answer to the above question. If people are left free to seek truth for themselves, so the argument goes, then each will come up with his own private truth based on his narrow understanding or personal self-interests, and moral anarchy will ensue. Better an enforced uniformity, even if superficial, than a creative chaos.

The problem with this argument is its assumption that the multiplicity and diversity of seekers will necessarily result in a multiplicity and diversity of truths. For if truth is one point (as the Bahá'í Writings repeatedly affirm), then all those who persist in seeking truth will sooner or later approach that point and thus draw near each to the other. This is an example of *convergence*, where the persistent (repeated) application of a process leads from different initial positions and by different paths to the same final position or target.[37]

---

37. In recent years, the mathematics of dynamical systems has yielded immense knowledge about, and many examples of, systems in which such convergence occurs. Indeed, we can now say that such convergent phenomena are more the rule than the exception in

For example, it is objectively true that all humans tend to respond positively to love and kindness, on one hand, and to respond negatively and aggressively to cruelty and mistreatment, on the other. If we all persist in pursuing autonomy and authenticity, then each of us will, in our own way and sooner or later, confront this objective truth in a manner that leads us voluntarily to relinquish our selfish and aggressive behavior towards others. We will clearly perceive that we are literally creating our own unhappiness and destroying our own well-being by treating others (or ourselves) in a inauthentic manner.

Supporters of the argumen in favor of uniformity usually invoke the history of doctrinal conflict in religion as evidence for the implausibility (or at least the impracticality) of a true convergence resulting from a *multi-autonomous* search for truth (i.e., where each individual pursues the truth in the way he or she personally and freely chooses). Our history certainly does furnish numerous examples of social conflicts resulting from doctrinal differences between various belief systems. But this history would be evidence against the viability of multi-autonomy *only if* these conflicts actually resulted from a genuine multi-autonomous search for truth in which each came up with a different truth. However, an examination of the historical circumstances of doctrinal conflicts tends to show rather that such conflicts arose precisely because the individuals involved had, at some point, abandoned the search for truth and instead capitulated their autonomous judgment in favor of blind belief in an ideology. One cannot therefore reasonably view such conflicts as resulting from genuine multi-autonomous truth-seeking.

This naturally raises the question as to why so few people in our history seem to have persisted in the path of autonomous truth-seeking. The answer to this question is complex and many-faceted. In the first place, autonomous truth seeking involves a temporary, willful suspension of natural credulousness—the kind of deliberate doubt

---

nature. Were it otherwise, natural systems would be volatile, unstable, and ultimately self-destructive, given the immense diversity of conditions (starting points) under which such systems must function.

(or questioning) which Descartes describes so well.[38] But such questioning leads in turn to a certain non-negligible level of personal anxiety. Some find it difficult to endure this anxiety of uncertainty for very long, and become desperate to end it by simply handing over their judgment to some established ideology or belief system. The implicit bargain is: I will accept as true whatever you decree as long as you will relieve my anxieties by eliminating the uncertainties from my life.

There is a subtle point here that Descartes fully realized and articulated. This self-generated, deliberate doubt is not a willful indulgence of negative thinking and is quite different from skepticism, especially that arrogant and aggressive skepticism which looks with disdain on the beliefs of others. Deliberate doubt is an act of humility, not pride, and is directed towards ourselves, not others. It is an attempt to purify our inner model by focusing on the basis of belief—the process by which we come to hold anything as true—rather than only on the substance or content of belief. It seeks to implement Bahá'u'lláh's injunction to "cleanse [the] heart . . . from the obscuring dust of all acquired knowledge"[39] in the pursuit of authenticity.

The focus on process enables us to understand the dynamics of truth-seeking and therefore to progress continually in the discovery of truth. Single-minded focus only on the content of our beliefs may lead us to a static state in which we are comfortable with a certain limited worldview but unable to advance further in the path of truth-seeking.

In other words, even if we go through the exercise of self-examination only to end up with exactly the same set of beliefs as

---

38. René Descartes (1596–1650) was the philosopher and scientist who initiated the modern era by uniting in one creative conception the Western (Greek) tradition of geometry and the Eastern (Hindu-Arabic) tradition of algebra. In order to purify his philosophy from all acquired or historical prejudices, he began from a position of deliberate, universal doubt. He then proceeded by accepting only that which could not be reasonably negated by such doubt. His first conclusion was his own existence ("I think, therefore I am") and the second was the existence of God. Descartes' philosophy thus pioneered the use of systematic and deliberate doubt as a method for attaining to truth.

39. Bahá'u'lláh, Gleanings, p. 264.

before, the exercise is valuable because now we are aware of the basis of our beliefs. We know not only what we believe but why we believe it. This knowledge of the basis or justification for our beliefs is essential to the achievement of autonomy and thus of authenticity.

However, once the process of self-examination and scrutiny of the basis of belief is started, there is no turning back. We can abandon the process, but we can never return to the innocence of our pre-examination unawareness. Perhaps, then, this is a second reason why so few people seem to have persisted in the path of autonomy: there is no *a priori* guarantee that we will find answers to our questions. There is thus the fear of getting stuck in the questioning stage, unable to emerge from it.

This is where the "will to truth" discussed in chapter 2 is so important. At some point in our lives, we must throw caution to the wind and decide that we want to know the truth above all else, no matter at what cost. This means accepting the *logical possibility* (not the plausibility) of nihilism—that there is no truth to be found. Once we have dared to stare pure nonbeing in the face and realize that it is an illusion, we acquire a new and deep certitude of the objective existence of moral and spiritual realities, laws, forces, and entities.

It is admittedly difficult to conceive how God has managed to create the human reality in such manner that the process of establishing an ordered and just society is compatible with the individual pursuit of autonomy and authenticity. Ultimately, this compatibility rests on one fundamental reality: the objectivity of the causality relationship, which means that there are objective consequences to every action we initiate. Thus, if we each continually seek to optimize our autonomy and well-being, we will all converge towards the same objective reality in spite of the diversity of our initial starting points or the individual differences in the paths we may follow.

A social order based on the multi-autonomous pursuit of authenticity will actually be more stable and enduring (and certainly more dynamic) than would be the same order if based on an externally enforced uniformity. The very fact that authentic morality is based on conscious self-motivation, rather than on a grudging fear of the social consequences of immorality, will enable future society to divert its collective energies from strategies for controlling the masses to strategies for increasing the well-being and autonomy of all.

The following three diagrams illustrate, respectively, the asymmetry of power-based relations, the rigid equality of a socially enforced uniformity, and the dynamic reciprocity of authentic morality.

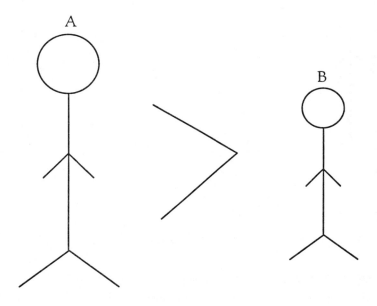

Fig. 3.3. Representation of the asymmetry of power-based relations

Relationships based on powerseeking and competitive behavior lead inevitably to a "win-lose" configuration in which one of the parties, A, dominates or oppresses the other, B. In the absence of social controls this leads to anarchy (every person for himself) and in the presence of social controls yields a highly volatile and unstable order, requiring immense inputs of energy to prevent the collapse of the system.

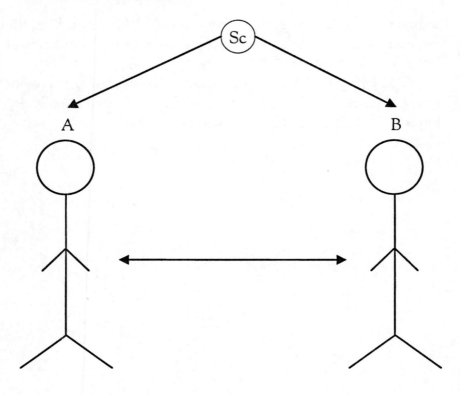

Fig. 3.4. Representation of the configuration of socially-enforced uniformity

This diagram gives a schematic representation of the configuration of socially-enforced uniformity. Individuals A and B receive their value or status from the society as a whole, Sc, which decrees a rigid equality of moral status between them. This is generally a "lose-lose" situation where everyone is equally oppressed by an authoritarian structure.

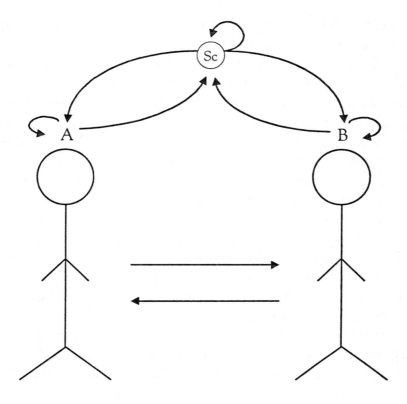

Fig. 3.5. Representation of the ideal configuration of autonomous authenticity

This diagram represents the ideal configuration towards which autonomous authenticity converges. First, there is the reflexive relationship of each member of society to himself or herself. This is the
recognition of one's own intrinsic value, the inner relationship between the self and God. Next, there is the mutual recognition of
intrinsic value between any two members of society, A and B. Since
mutual value recognition generates mutual love, this is a "win-win"
configuration where each experiences the joy of both giving and
receiving love. There is also a mutual, dynamic relationship between
each individual and society as a whole, Sc. Finally, there is the collective recognition of the intrinsic value of society itself, both as the
sum of individual intrinsic values and as providing a just order which
fosters the authentic well-being and autonomy of each individual

member. This is the concept of "unity in diversity" repeatedly mentioned in the Bahá'í Writings.

Thus, the trademark of authentic morality is that it genuinely seeks the moral autonomy and conscious self-motivation of every individual. Moreover, authentic morality affirms that every human being has the capacity and potential to become morally autonomous. Finally, authentic morality asserts that the universal, multi-autonomous pursuit of authenticity converges to a stable but dynamic configuration of society as a whole, a configuration that has never yet been realized in our history because of the predominance of inauthentic pursuits.

In thinking about the relationship between the external social order on one hand and individual moral autonomy on the other, a further, extremely important point should be stressed. The morally autonomous individual does not exalt his or her conscience above the considered judgment of those collective institutions invested with legitimate moral authority. Such institutions are absolutely necessary, not only to establish social order, but more importantly to provide a framework of justice which allows and encourages individuals to seek genuine moral autonomy. Without such institutions, multi-autonomy will simply never exist in the first place.

Of course, once we realize the objectivity of multi-autonomous moral convergence, it is tempting to conclude that an ideal society could be achieved spontaneously, i.e., without the establishment of morally authoritative institutions. If it were the case that every individual human being spontaneously arose to pursue moral authenticity, there might in fact be no need for such institutions. But our history has shown us that at most a handful of individuals in each generation will arise spontaneously to pursue authenticity. If the prevailing social order and the existing social structures do not favor and encourage authenticity, then the vast majority of individuals will be unable to resist the temptation to the various substitutions for authenticity: sexual promiscuity, money, power, and the various instant gratifications of the pleasure instinct such as drugs and alcohol.

Among the minimal, necessary social prerequisites for generalized multi-autonomy are: stable and loving families; an authentic and structured system of moral education for children, undertaken first by parents and, then gradually, by the other institutions of society; social structures that favor cooperation and sharing rather than competition and conflict; an economic system that is (and is perceived to be) just and which eliminates the extremes of wealth and poverty. These structural conditions cannot and will never arise spontaneously, nor can they be conceived and implemented by individuals acting alone, however creative or autonomous such individuals may be. They must be carefully built and implemented under the guidance of morally legitimate social institutions.

Moreover, such a social project requires the synergy of group consultation and other healthy group processes. Social institutions based on cooperation and sharing cannot come forth fully born from a society based on conflict and competition. Rather they must come forth from a *process* by which cooperation and sharing are gradually increased (convergence again). In the absence of a morally legitimate social authority, the conception and implementation of such processes will be impossible.

Thus, the objectivity of multi-autonomous convergence does not allow us to disregard structural issues, because without the proper social structures, genuine autonomy and thus genuine convergence will simply never occur. But the reality of convergence does give us the necessary basis on which to build a society that is both ordered and dynamic, rather than just ordered by an externally imposed uniformity.

11. Moral Dilemmas

The system of ethics we have presented is based not on rules but on principles. A rule dictates exactly how one should act in a given circumstance. A principle gives the moral goal that is sought and the nature of the action necessary to attain the goal, but it does not absolutely determine the action to be taken. For example, if you thoughtlessly insult or offend me, then you have violated the principle of altruistic love. This same principle dictates that I should respond in a manner that will increase the probability that our future interactions will be more harmonious, but nevertheless does not determine a unique response on my part. That is, even when I have resolved to act on the basis of the principle, I still have a certain freedom of choice as to how I will undertake to do so.

Thus, a principle-based ethical system usually "underdetermines" the individual's response in a given circumstance, leaving room for creativity in the pursuit of moral development. This makes morality a positive and dynamic process, and not just a negative process of avoiding "wrongdoing."

Of course, in many situations there may well be a minimum morally acceptable response. (For example, in the circumstance described above, I should, in no case, respond by insulting you in retaliation to your insult.) However, there will rarely if ever be a maximum response. Thus, no matter how creative and positive my response, I may, under similar circumstances in the future, find an even better one. The pursuit of authentic morality thus becomes a creative process of continual development and growth.

Even though a principle-based ethical system does not always determine a unique proper response, the particular circumstances of a given interaction may nonetheless practically determine the response. (If you are a stranger who has insulted me on the bus, I do not have the option of bringing you a cup of tea and talking over our relationship.) However, a sufficiently complex interaction may bring into play different principles which appear equally applicable to the circumstances of the interaction but which suggest different responses. In this case, the response is "overdetermined." We are then faced with a *moral dilemma*.

In a rule-based system, a moral dilemma may constitute a genuine contradiction in that strict application of the rules will require me to accomplish mutually exclusive or logically impossible actions. The flexibility of a coherent, principle-based system like ours avoids explicit contradictions, but can nonetheless result in some difficult dilemmas.

Suppose, for example, that we are in a group situation (among close friends, say) and I hear you tell a lie to the group. Should I denounce the lie to the group, or not? The spontaneous response of most people to this dilemma is to say that no, I should not denounce the lie to the group. I can speak with you privately afterwards if I feel that justice requires me to confront you. In this way, the unity of the group is maintained and you are not needlessly humiliated in public.

However, suppose that your lie gives critically false information that others may act upon to their detriment or even serious harm. Then I must denounce the lie to protect innocent parties from being victimized. I can, of course, attempt to correct the false information without making it seem that you have deliberately misled others, but if, for example, you force the issue, then I have no other authentic choice but to establish the truth in the eyes of everyone. In this case, it will then be your own action that has discredited you. Nevertheless, depending on the circumstances, it may take considerable moral courage on my part to respond in an authentic manner. It could, for example, put our friendship into jeopardy, or, depending on our relationship and the reason for your lie, expose me to future attempts on your part to punish me or sabotage my life in some manner.

In resolving a moral dilemma, we can do no better than to evaluate carefully the various elements of the interaction, to determine the predominant principle, and then to act accordingly. We will not always succeed, even when trying our best, nor will we always have the time to engage in extensive reflection before acting. However, what we discover is that actions which were initially difficult and self-conscious gradually become habitual and finally instinctive. As 'Abdu'l-Bahá has assured us:

> It is possible to so adjust one's self to the practice of nobility that its atmosphere surrounds and colors all our acts. When these acts are habitually and conscientiously adjusted to noble standards with no thought of the words that might herald them,

then nobility becomes the accent of life. At such a degree of evolution one scarcely needs to try to be good any longer—all our deeds are the distinctive expression of nobility.[40]

Thus, there are pitfalls and dilemmas that await us in our moral striving, but also the reward of increasingly authentic relationships, of continually heightened autonomy, and of a stable and enduring well-being. We must therefore strive to maintain the higher view and the broader perspective whenever we are in the midst of our struggle. We cannot succeed unless we are firmly convinced and inwardly resolved that our attempts to act morally constitute the only true and ultimate meaning of our life.

---

40. 'Abdu'l-Bahá, *Star of the West*, vol. 17, p. 286.

Appendix I

Brief Axiomatic Sketch of the Principal Concepts of the System of Authentic Morality

Definitions

1. By *reality* we mean the totality of all existence, everything there is (or was or will be).

2. A *proposition* is a statement (in some given language) which makes an affirmation (assertion) about how some portion of reality is configured.

3. A *theory* is a collection of propositions (in the same language).

4. A *belief* is a proposition to which we attach a certain value.

5. A *belief system* is a collection of beliefs.

6. An *ideology* is a belief system which attributes to certain of its propositions a value greater than the human being.

Main Axioms and Corollaries

Axiom 1. The human being is the supreme value (in creation).

Axiom 2. The value of the human being is intrinsic (to the essential nature of the human being) and universal (shared by every human being).

Axiom 3. Higher values are ends and lower values are means.

> Corollary 1. We should always use lesser values as means to the end of obtaining higher values. We should therefore never sacrifice a higher value to obtain a lower value.

> Corollary 2. Morality (the implementation of moral values) consists in the pursuit of authentic human relationships.

> Corollary 3. Any ideology is false since, by definition, an ideology considers human beings inferior to certain doctrines and thus considers it legitimate that human beings and/or authentic human relationships be sacrificed (made a means) for the promulgation of these doctrines.

Axiom 4. Human behavior is determined primarily by our perception of reality rather than by reality itself.

> Corollary 4. If we do not perceive the human being as the supreme value, then we will use others as means to our ends (in spite of the objective truth of Axiom 1).

Axiom 5. The human being is capable of both extreme cruelty and extreme altruism.

> Corollary 5. We cannot act cruelly towards others if we truly perceive them as the supreme value in creation.

Appendix II

Sketch of Formalized Version of the Proof of the Existence of God

For those who have some familiarity with formal logic, we consider here a more formal, step by step version of our proof of God's existence presented in chapter 3 (pp. 82–86). We hereby assume without modification the various definitions and principles of chapter 3, section 4. Let us begin with a clear statement of what we are trying to prove.

Desired Conclusion: There exists a unique self-caused noncomposite entity G which is a universal cause. To say that G is a universal cause means precisely that, for every phenomenon A, $G \rightarrow A$.

First step: definition of the global phenomenon V

Definition of V. V is the universe (collection) of all entities. Thus, every entity A is a component of V, $A \in V$.

Comment on Definition of V. In fact, since V is the collection of *all* entities, it follows that *to be an entity is to be a component of V*. Or stated another way, to be an entity is to be a component, and so *a phenomenon A is a component if and only if it is a component of V*. V is thus the collection of all components of all systems. Thus, all components A of any system B are components of V. But this means that

139

every composite phenomenon B is a subsystem of V, B ⊂ V. Hence, every phenomenon B is either an entity (and thus a component of V, B ∈ V) or else a subsystem of V, B ⊂ V. In particular V ⊂ V, V is a subsystem of itself (which does *not* mean that V is a component of itself!).

Next step: what is the status of V with regards to causality?

Theorem 1. V is not self-caused.

Proof

We now ask the question "can V be self-caused, V → V?" Well, let us suppose it were (we are seeking a contradiction), i.e., suppose V → V. Then, by the potency principle, V → A, where A is any component of V. But this contradicts the principle of limitation, which says that no composite can be the cause of one of its own components. But how do we know that, in fact, V *has* components, i.e., that it is composite? Well, suppose that V has no components. Then there are no entities, and therefore no non-empty systems, because all components of systems are entities by definition. But we know from simple, direct observation that non-empty systems do exist (this piece of paper you are reading, for example). Thus, entities exist and V is composite. Hence V is not self-caused.

Conclusion from Theorem 1

The principle of sufficient reasons tells us that every phenomenon must be either self-caused or other-caused. Since V is not self-caused it must be other-caused by some phenomen G, G → V, G ≠ V. But, we have already seen above that every phenomenon is either a component or a subsystem of V. Thus, G itself is either a subsystem or a component of V, G ∈ V, or G ⊂ V. Whichever is the case, the potency principle tells us that G → G. Thus, G is self-caused and hence cannot be composite, by an argument similar to the one we applied above to show that V is composite and thus not self-caused.

Thus, G is a non-composite phenomenon and hence an entity.

Furthermore, since every phenomenon B is either a component or a subsystem of V, then the potency principle tells us once again that $G \to B$. Hence G is a non-composite, self-caused, universal cause. It remains only to show that G is unique.

Suppose there were another universal cause G'. Then $G \to G'$ since G is universal. But G' is also universal and hence self-caused, $G' \to G'$. Thus, G' cannot be other-caused (principle of sufficient reason). Thus the cause G of G' must be G' itself, i.e., $G = G'$. We have thus reached our desired conclusion. (In fact, we have also shown that G is the only self-caused phenomenon in existence.) Notice also that once a self-caused entity $G \to G$ exists, it is eternal since its own existence is a sufficient reason for its continued existence.

Final Comments

Notice that we have used every one of our three principles in deriving this conclusion. Moreover, none of our principles directly posits the existence of anything. The only extralogical assumption we have used is our explicit appeal to the fact that something exists. We have thus showed that if anything exists, then God (a universal, uncaused cause) exists.

Of course, some might contend that our three logical principles are abstract and thus not subject to direct verification and hence open to question. However, rejecting one or another of those principles is not such a simple matter as might as first be supposed, because to deny any proposition is to affirm that its negation (denial) is true. Moreover, each of our three principles is a universal statement, whose negation is thus an existential statement, i.e., a statement that affirms the necessary existence of an entity or system satisfying certain highly implausible conditions.

For example, if the principle of limitation be denied, then we are committed to belief in the objective existence of some system which *is in fact* the cause of one of its own components. The existence of such a system is highly implausible and has certainly never been observed.

A similar remark applies to the other two principles, sufficient reason and potency. We have elsewhere called such principles "empirically grounded" because they are metaphysical extrapolations from observational truths (facts).

This shows that *nihilistic atheism*—the denial of the existence of any abstract, objectively existing entities that satisfy nonobservable conditions—is logically untenable.

Appendix III

The Virtuous Cycle

'Abdu'l-Bahá has said that absolute stasis is impossible in this life; at every instant we are either progressing or retrogressing:

> Absolute repose does not exist in nature. All things either make progress or lose ground. Everything moves forward or backward, nothing is without motion. . . .
>
> The world of mortality is a world of contradictions, of opposites; motion being compulsory everything must either go forward or retreat. . . .
>
> My hope for you is that you will progress in the world of spirit, as well as in the world of matter; that your intelligence will develop, your knowledge will augment, and your understanding be widened.
>
> You must ever press forward, never standing still; avoid stagnation, the first step to a backward movement, to decay.[1]

Thus, whether we like it or not, throughout our adult life we are in the process of choosing, on the one hand, the pursuit of authenticity, moving forward toward increased moral autonomy and spiritual well-being, or, on the other hand, the pursuit of power, moving backwards towards morbid dependencies and spiritual degeneracy. More-

---

1. 'Abdu'l-Bahá, *Paris Talks*, nos. 29:2, 29:9, and 29:10–11.

over, as 'Abdu'l-Bahá has indicated in the passage quoted above, we cannot avoid choosing. The refusal to choose is itself a choice. Not to press forward proactively is to retrogress. As Shoghi Effendi has put it:

> Life is a constant struggle, not only against forces around us, but above all against our own ego. We can never afford to rest on our oars, for if we do, we soon see ourselves carried down stream again.[2]

In other words, underlying the process of moral development is an entropy principle quite similar to the second law of thermodynamics[3] in physics: *There are always more wrong ways than right ways to do anything. Thus, it is easier to do things wrong than to do them right.* Indeed, the "right" ways lead to more refined, less probable configurations, and are therefore fewer than the virtually unlimited number of ways of producing moral failure. In fact, the easiest thing to do is nothing and that is always wrong as we have seen in the above quotations from the Bahá'í Writings.

So, the most basic truth of the process of spiritual transformation is the fact that we are compelled to act: change, not stasis, is the norm. But, knowing that we must act does not, in itself, tell us how to act. Acting effectively and self-responsibly to bring about *constructive* change involves at least the following essential elements: (1) a clear conception of our present condition, of where we currently stand; (2) a clear conception of the goal or ideal condition we seek to obtain, of where we want to go; (3) a well-conceived, staged process that, if implemented properly, will clearly lead us from where we are to where we want to be; and, (4) a motivation that is strong enough to sustain this transitional process and overcome whatever obstacles we encounter in the course of its prosecution.

---

2. Shoghi Effendi, *Unfolding Destiny*, p. 454.

3. The second law of thermodynamics states that heat will not move from a lower temperature to a higher one without the intervention of some outside source. It can also be articulated as the principal that, in an isolated system, entropy (disorder) never decreases over time. Simply stated: Order is improbable and disorder is probable.

On the basis of the fundamental concepts contained in the text of *Love, Power, and Justice,* a generic model for such a transformational process has been developed by an interdisciplinary team of researchers. Now named the Authenticity Project, this team has met regularly for a period of several years and generated a substantial quantity of materials for the application and implementation of the basic concepts of *Love, Power, and Justice.*[4] These materials are being gradually refined through a series of seminars and courses, and the intention is to publish them when they will have reached a sufficiently mature stage of development.

The heart of the Authenticity Model for self-transformation is a six-step process called "the virtuous cycle."[5] This newly added third appendix to the second edition of *Love, Power, and Justice* presents, at least in outline, the currently developed form of the virtuous cycle. The team feels this gesture is timely, even though work on the virtuous cycle is not yet complete.

The Steps of the Virtuous Cycle

As we go through the steps of the virtuous cycle, it is important to recall that the defining characteristic of human nature is consciousness, or self-awareness, and that the basic capacities of the human soul are mind, heart, and will. The successful prosecution of each successive step in the virtuous cycle necessitates the coordinated application of all our basic capacities and involves an increase in both the scope and depth of our consciousness. It also involves a gradual increase in autonomy and self-mastery.

The six steps of the virtuous cycle fall naturally into three stages, each with two steps. The first stage represents a subprocess of prepar-

---

4. The so-called core group of the Authenticity Project is currently comprised of Leslie Asplund, Carmel Davey-Hatcher, Sheri Dressler, William Hatcher, Lonya Osokin, Michael Penn, and Mary K. Radpour.

5. The name "virtuous cycle" for the process of constructive change was deliberately chosen in opposition to the well-known term "vicious cycle," used to described the cycle of increasing dependencies and compulsive self-destruction often associated with morally and psychologically pathological behaviors and attitudes.

ing for change, the second a subprocess of formulating a plan for change, and the third stage consists of implementing the change for which we have prepared and planned.

We begin the whole cycle by focusing on some particular configuration (situation) in our lives about which we are currently concerned.

Stage I. Preparation for Constructive Change

Step 1. Investigating Current Reality

We begin by a deliberate attempt to increase our awareness of the present condition both of our selves and our environment. We seek facts, perceptions, observations, and descriptions. We ask ourselves "what" questions. In particular, we try to become aware of what we are currently thinking (mind) and feeling (heart).

- What am I currently thinking about this situation? Is this familiar or strange and new? What interpersonal relationships are primarily affecting or contributing to this situation? What are the others involved saying and doing about this situation?

- What am I currently feeling about the situation? Is this comfortable? Have I felt this way before? Do I feel mostly positive, negative, or ambivalent about the situation?

We also try to identify clearly our current motivations, desires, and actions (will).

- What are my current goals, and how am I acting to achieve them? What are my needs and desires? How am I behaving in this situation? Have I behaved this way before? Do I want to change?

Step 2. Gaining Insight and Understanding

We seek explanations, interpretations, and causes for the facts enumerated in step 1. We seek patterns of relationships between and among these facts. We ask "why" and "how" questions, thus going beyond perceptions to conceptions, and beyond descriptions to theories. We seek to understand the point(s) of view (inner model(s)) underlying the observed facts.

- What is the most reasonable hypothesis concerning the mental conceptions underlying the observed behavior, both in myself and others (why are we acting as we do)? What assumptions are we making about each other (how do we conceive one another)? Are these assumptions reasonable or unreasonable, conscious or unconscious?

- What are the (possibly unconscious) feelings and attitudes most likely to have produced the observed behavior? What feelings and attitudes are reflected in the behavior? What feelings and attitudes tend to be generated by the behavior (how do my actions make others feel)?

- What ends does the observed behavior really tend to serve (regardless of the stated or presumed intention)? What desires appear to motivate the behavior (what is the "payoff" or reward sought by each person)? What needs or desires are fulfilled by the behavior?

Stage II. Formulating a Plan for Constructive Change

Step 3. Envisioning What Could and Should Be

We envision the ideal of what could be (the possible) and what should be (the desirable), and compare our understanding of the current reality (step 2) with that ideal. We now ask value questions; we ask "which" questions. We morally evaluate the current reality, judging and assessing it in the light of an ideal standard of values and virtues.

- Which values and virtues are present in the current situation?

Which are absent? If the situation were ideal, what characteristics would it have? How would my point of view (inner model) be different if I were functioning in an ideal manner? Which elements of the current situation represent an authentic relationship to self and others (i.e., a relationship based on an accurate understanding of reality and a genuine concern for human well-being), and which elements are clearly inauthentic? 'Abdu'l-Bahá has said that any given condition of wrongdoing or pathology (inauthenticity) is due to some combination of ignorance (lack of understanding), immaturity (lack of development), or sickness (improper development). Which of these factors predominates in the current situation?

- How would I feel in the ideal situation? Am I currently attracted to these ideal feelings? Am I capable of giving myself to such feelings and, if not, what fears might I need to face? What attitudes towards others should I have in the ideal situation? Which attitudes would be more authentic?

- How do I see myself acting in the ideal situation? How would my actions in the ideal situation differ from my present actions?

Step 4. Selecting a Plan of Action
From among the various possible ideal configurations, we select a plan of action that we will seek to implement concretely and practically.

- Which higher values do I choose to implement with regards to this situation? Among the virtues and values lacking in the present situation (and which we have identified in step 3), which seem to be the most needed? Which virtue, if implemented, has the greatest potential for effecting significant constructive change? Which virtue or virtues are the most realizable in the light of (1) the needs of the current situation and (2) the inner, spiritual resources (including prayer and reliance on God) that

I possess or can acquire within a reasonable length of time? What practical steps can I take towards implementing the values and virtues I have chosen?

We must keep in mind that it is unrealistic to expect that we can move, in one step, from a relatively low level of authentic functioning to a relatively high level without passing through the intermediate stages. It is therefore better to be realistic about our expectations and accomplish some genuine progress than to pursue an unrealistically high ideal and fail completely.

Stage III. Implementing the Plan for Change

Step 5. Identifying and Anticipating Barriers to Change
We strive to anticipate those conditions of our lives most likely to challenge our intent to change. We ask mainly "how" questions.

- How can I prepare to face and overcome my own resistance to the contemplated change? How can I prepare to face others' resistance to my making this change?

- What perceptions of myself might I have to relinquish in order to make this change? What reactions to my changed behavior do I anticipate from others? With the help of God, how can I generate the degree of love and humility necessary to accomplish the contemplated action and to sustain the resulting change?

- How much resistance do I feel to making this change? What losses will I experience by making this change? What feelings about myself will I have to give up in order to make this change?

- Do I have the courage to actualize the given virtue in the circumstances, regardless of the anticipated reaction of others? Am I ready to "own" my actions—to take responsibility for their consequences? What, precisely, is my intention in executing the contemplated action? What do I expect to happen or want to happen?

- What kind of internal and external support do I need to help me sustain this change?

Step 6. Executing the Action, then Evaluating the Reaction

We now execute the contemplated action with as much awareness, deliberateness, and naturalness as possible. We then evaluate the results of having done this.

- How effectively did I accomplish my intention? What was the reaction of others? What was my own reaction? What thoughts went through my mind as I acted? What seemed to be the thoughts of others? What emotions did I feel as I accomplished my action? What seemed to be the emotions experienced by others? Do I feel rather good or rather bad? Why? Has the situation now moved closer to what could or should be as analyzed in step 3?

What is the new situation as a result of my action? This situation now constitutes the current reality. We therefore loop to step 1 and iterate (repeat) the virtuous cycle process.

Comments and Conclusions

We have articulated the steps of the virtuous cycle in the most general terms possible in order to underline its universality. It can be used to make a simple decision and to solve a very specific, concrete problem, or to make a momentous decision and resolve a major life crisis, or to effect proactively some major change in one's life and in oneself.

A more complete explication and elaboration of the steps of the virtuous cycle will show that it is an intricate combination of spiritual principles contained in the Bahá'í Writings, on the one hand,

and basic concepts of modern psychology, on the other. Indeed, one of the major insights deriving from the work of the Authenticity Project is the realization that the purely logical principles governing the process of psychotherapy are essentially the same as the principles underlying the process of spiritual and moral development (self-transformation). The main differences in the ways we may experience the virtuous cycle lie in our initial condition, when we first engage the process. If we are highly dysfunctional, we will most likely need professional help until we achieve a certain degree of autonomy in the application of the principles of the virtuous cycle. If, however, we are fortunate enough to have had a solid moral education as children and youth, we may be able to engage the virtuous cycle proactively on our own.

However, in either case, the nature of the tests and challenges of life are such that we will all need to help and encourage each other if we are to be successful. The personal experience of any individual life is limited, and we can each absorb only a finite quantity of direct experience. So we each have much to learn from the experience of others.

Shoghi Effendi has observed that "Ultimately all the battle of life is within the individual."[6] Thus, prosecution of the virtuous cycle is primarily a responsibility of the individual. Nevertheless, the virtuous cycle has an important collective and social dimension. It presupposes an immense degree of cooperative (noncompetitive) sharing between individuals at different stages of development.

In more general terms, those social structures which foster cooperation and mutuality naturally provide a social space or atmosphere that is more conducive to the individual pursuit of the virtuous cycle than a negative environment rooted in continual conflict and strife. As Shoghi Effendi is reported to have stated: "The whole object of our lives is bound up with the lives of all human beings; not a personal salvation we are seeking, but a universal one. . . . Our aim

---

6. On behalf of Shoghi Effendi, from a letter dated December 18, 1943 to an individual believer, in *Living the Life: A Compilation*, p. 20.

is to produce a world civilization which will in turn react on the character of the individual."[7]

Of course, what we have presented here is only the barest outline of the essentials of the virtuous cycle. Moreover, there is, as always in such matters, an immense difference between a purely intellectual understanding of the virtuous cycle and the ability to implement that understanding successfully. It is to facilitate the acquisition of this ability that the materials of the Authenticity Project are dedicated.

---

7. Ruḥiyyih Khánúm, "To the Baháʼí Youth," *Baháʼí News*, no. 231 (May 1950): p. 6.

Bibliography

Writings of Bahá'u'lláh

Gleanings from the Writings of Bahá'u'lláh. 1st ps. ed. Translated by Shoghi Effendi.
   Wilmette, Ill.: Bahá'í Publishing Trust, 1983.
The Hidden Words. Translated by Shoghi Effendi. Wilmette, Ill.: Bahá'í Publishing Trust,
   1939.
The Kitáb-i-Aqdas: The Most Holy Book. ps. ed. Wilmette, Ill.: Bahá'í Publishing Trust,
   1993.
The Seven Valleys and Four Valleys. New ed. Translated by Marzieh Gail and Ali-Kuli
   Khan. Wilmette, Ill.: Bahá'í Publishing Trust, 1991.
Tablets of Bahá'u'lláh revealed after the Kitáb-i-Aqdas. 1st ps. ed. Compiled by the Research
   Department of the Universal House of Justice. Translated by Habib Taherzadeh et
   al. Wilmette, Ill.: Bahá'í Publishing Trust, 1988.

Writings of 'Abdu'l-Bahá

Paris Talks: Addresses Given by 'Abdu'l-Bahá in Paris in 1911. 12th ed. London: Bahá'í
   Publishing Trust, 1995.
The Promulgation of Universal Peace: Talks Delivered by 'Abdu'l-Bahá during His Visit to the
   United States and Canada in 1912. 2d. ed. Compiled by Howard MacNutt.
   Wilmette, Ill.: Bahá'í Publishing Trust, 1982.
The Secret of Divine Civilization. 1st ps. ed. Translated by Marzieh Gail and Ali-Kuli Khan.
   Wilmette, Ill.: Bahá'í Publishing Trust, 1990.
Selections from the Writings of 'Abdu'l-Bahá. 1st ps. ed. Compiled by the Research Depart-
   ment of the Universal House of Justice. Translated by a Committee at the Bahá'í
   World Centre and Marzieh Gail. Wilmette, Ill.: Bahá'í Publishing Trust, 1997.

Writings of Shoghi Effendi

Advent of Divine Justice. 1st ps. ed. Wilmette, Ill.: Bahá'í Publishing Trust, 1990.

The Bahá'í Life: Extracts from the Letters and Writings of Shoghi Effendi. 1st U.S. ed. Compiled by the Universal House of Justice. Wilmette, Ill.: Bahá'í Publishing Trust, 1981.

The Dispensation of Bahá'u'lláh. London: Bahá'í Publishing Trust, 1947.

The Unfolding Destiny of the British Bahá'í Community: The Messages from the Guardian of the Bahá'í Faith to the Bahá'ís of the British Isles. London: Bahá'í Publishing Trust, 1981.

The World Order of Bahá'u'lláh. 1st ps. ed. Wilmette, Ill.: Bahá'í Publishing Trust, 1991.

Writings of the Universal House of Justice

Messages from the Universal House of Justice, 1963–1986: The Third Epoch of the Formative Age. Compiled by Geoffry Marks. Wilmette, Ill.: Bahá'í Publishing Trust, 1996.

The Promise of World Peace: To the Peoples of the World. Wilmette, Ill.: Bahá'í Publishing Trust, 1985.

Compilations of Bahá'í Writings

Bahá'u'lláh and 'Abdu'l-Bahá. *Bahá'í World Faith: Selected Writings of Bahá'u'lláh and 'Abdu'l-Bahá.* 2d ed. Wilmette, Ill.: Bahá'í Publishing Trust, 1976.

Bahá'u'lláh, 'Abdu'l-Bahá, and Shoghi Effendi. *Spiritual Foundations: Prayer, Meditation, and the Devotional Attitude: Extracts from the Writings of Bahá'u'lláh, 'Abdu'l-Bahá, and Shoghi Effendi.* Compiled by the Research Department of the Universal House of Justice. Wilmette, Ill.: Bahá'í Publishing Trust, 1980.

Bahá'u'lláh, the Báb, and 'Abdu'l-Bahá. *Bahá'í Prayers: A Selection of Prayers Revealed by Bahá'u'lláh, the Báb, and 'Abdu'l-Bahá.* New ed. Wilmette, Ill.: Bahá'í Publishing Trust, 1991.

Shoghi Effendi and the Universal House of Justice. *Living the Life: A Compilation.* London: Bahá'í Publishing Trust, 1974.

Other Works

Bahá'í News. No. 231. May 1950.

Grundy, Julia M. *Ten Days in the Light of 'Akká.* Rev. ed. Wilmette, Ill.: Bahá'í Publishing Trust, 1979.

Hatcher, John S. and William S. Hatcher. *The Law of Love Enshrined: Selected Essays.* Oxford: George Ronald, 1996.

Hatcher, William S. *Logic and Logos: Essays on Science, Religion and Philosophy.* Oxford: George Ronald, 1990.

Leakey, R., and R. Lewin. *People of the Lake.* New York: Doubleday, 1978.

MacIntyre, Alastair. *After Virtue: A Study in Moral Theory.* Notre Dame, In.: University of Notre Dame Press, 1981.

Plato. *The Republic.* New York: Random House, 1981.

Poole, Ross. *Morality and Modernity.* London: Routledge, 1991.

Index